Bitting

IN THEORY AND PRACTICE

Elwyn Hartley Edwards

J A ALLEN
London

British Library Cataloguing in Publication Data
A catalogue record for this book is available from the British
Library

First edition published 1990
Reprinted 1993

Published in Great Britain by
J. A. Allen & Company Limited
1 Lower Grosvenor Place
London SW1W 0EL

ISBN 0-85131-527-5

Book production Bill Ireson

Printed in Great Britain by St Edmundsbury Press Limited,
Bury St Edmunds, Suffolk

Bitting

IN THEORY AND PRACTICE

Contents

List of Illustrations

This book, the second in the J. A. Allen Saddlery trilogy, is for all those delightful and very brave young ladies of the Pony Club and riding clubs who have been good enough, over the years, to let me think I could teach them anything about horses.

1: The Development of Bits and Bitting

Once people had embarked upon the domestication of animals larger and more powerful than themselves, they had, of necessity, to devise means of controlling those animals if they were going to be of use as a means of transport or of carrying loads.

Dogs, who head the domestication charts, threw in their lot with the human race about 12000 BC. As carnivores and natural pack animals, they were man's obvious auxiliary in his hunting forays and for that purpose no physical control was necessary.

Three thousand years later, sheep were kept in flocks by pastoral peoples, and two thousand years after that goats and pigs were added to the list. The only control required for groups of animals like these was a child with a stick, and initially herding would have implied no more than 'following' the wanderings of wild or semi-wild flocks as they grazed.

That was probably the case with reindeer also, which, being migratory animals, followed the path of the 'reindeer moss' on which they relied for their sustenance.

There is archaeological evidence to suggest that reindeer were pulling sledges in northern Europe as early as 5000 BC, and it seems more than likely that the forebears of the Uryanchai of Mongolia, the archetypal reindeer people, rode tamed reindeer as they followed the herds. That implies the existence of a form of control. As reindeer are tractable animals and easily kept, this would probably have amounted to no more than a halter. When the horse later became domesticated in almost the same steppelands, it is reasonable to suppose that a similar halter, made from woven grasses and later from strips of leather, would quite quickly have replaced the elementary loop of rope round the neck.

The advantage of a halter is that it can be used to apply pressure on the nose and thus increase the degree of restraint. Fitted low enough, it acts like a drop noseband to cause a temporary interruption of the breathing accompanied by an inevitable lowering of the head. Once the mouth is held lower than the hand, control is immediately increased. From that point it is but a small step to a thong tied round the lower jaw so that it lies between the molar and incisor teeth over the area of gum known as the 'bars' of the mouth. Five thousand years later the American Indian was using just such an arrangement. The fact that only a single rein was used, at least in the early stages, was hardly a matter of much consequence. If it passed up the right side of the neck, turning to the right was easily enough accomplished, but horses quickly learn to turn the opposite way from a rein laid against the neck ('neck-reining') when that action is accompanied by a shift of the rider's weight in the required direction. The Arab rider of today still rides with a single rein attached to the horse's nose in the same fashion, and controls a camel in the same way. But then the Arab was a camel man long before he took up riding horses.

The first record of horse domestication occurs between five and six thousand years ago and is generally credited to the nomadic steppe people of Eurasia, probably Aryan tribes moving around the steppes bordering the Caspian and Black Seas. Possibly it was taking place contemporaneously in other areas too.

The more settled communities, in the valley lands of the Tigris and Euphrates, for instance, had access to cattle that were certainly domesticated some three thousand years before the horse. In those societies, then not acquainted with horses, oxen performed well enough in the early forms of draught and as load carriers. Later, following the invention of the wheel, Syrians, Egyptians and people living in Mesopotamia acquired horses and became chariot drivers. Initially, because of its greater availability, the onager was used in war chariots, and Sumerian art of the third millennium BC shows teams of four onagers, harnessed abreast, drawing two- and four-wheeled vehicles. The harness employed was virtually identical to that which had for centuries proved successful with oxen. Central to it was the yoke, which, though quite unsuited to the equine conformation, was in time adapted well enough for chariots to operate successfully over level ground. Chariot harness that was recognisably derived from the ox-yoke persisted into the Christian era and, indeed, is still to be seen today – the Bombay 'chariot rig' being a prime example.

Oxen, of course, can be guided by no more than a rope fastened round the horns and the appropriate application of an 'ash-plant'. A more satisfactory means of control is by a nose-rope threaded through the nasal septum, or by a cord attached to a ring through the nose.

The same principle was applied to the onager, and Sumerian artefacts show teams being driven by reins attached to nose-rings or to rings passed through the upper lip and kept in place by a strap fastened under the jaw.

There is some evidence that horses were also controlled in this fashion in North Africa. Strabo, the Greek geographer, mentions the use of such a method, but it was hardly widespread or long-lasting; neither was the ill-tempered onager used for very long once horses became more easily available.

In the centuries on either side of the Christian era, North African horsemen, particularly the Numidians, managed to ride horses without any sort of bridle, 'plying a light switch between their horses' ears', as we are told by Silius Italicus. People in that part of the world still ride donkeys in the same way, but, of course, this would not do for a team of four horses galloping in a war chariot, when it was very necessary for the chariot crew to keep control over the situation.

The First Bits

Probably because the fear of sudden death at a headlong gallop can be wonderfully concentrating to the mind, a form of control and restraint appeared early on in our association with both the driven and the ridden horse. The halter and the thong round the lower jaw were quickly superseded by a bit, held in place across the lower jaw by a headpiece of leather or rope and, fairly soon, supported by a noseband, acting either independently or in conjunction with the bit.

Initially, bits may have been made from hardwood and then from bone and horn. These were certainly in use in Mesopotamia as early as 2300 BC, the approximate date when the horse replaced the less reliable onager. From 1300 to 1200 BC metal snaffles were in general use throughout the Near East. As the use of chariots and cavalry became more co-ordinated, so the bitting arrangements became more effective and even sophisticated. To manoeuvre a four-horse chariot at speed, or to command the cohesive movement of large concentrations of wheeled vehicles, which is even more difficult, individual animals must give an instant response to the reins if disaster is to be averted. Much depends on the training of the horses, but just as much on the efficiency of the controlling bit. (When the Hittites defeated the forces of Rameses I in the greatest 'armoured' conflict of the ancient world at Kadesh in 1286 BC, they did so by the co-ordinated use of no less than 3,500 chariots supported by 17,000 foot soldiers.)

Jointed snaffles, acting in a nutcracker action across the lower jaw and therefore much stronger in their effect than a straight mouthpiece, were in evidence almost from the outset. They were made sharper by incorporating a serrated mouthpiece, or one fitted with 'hedgehog' spikes, and the lateral effect was reinforced by cheeks or bit rings fitted with burrs that pricked into the sides of the cheeks.

The Teaching of Xenophon

The variations were endless but were, for the greater part, remarkably modern in appearance. No further important innovation was introduced until the fourth century BC when the Celts of Gaul introduced the curb bit, operating on the principle of levers – a mouthpiece that, in its essentials, has not changed very much since then. Xenophon (430–355 BC), that supremely gifted author of the first equestrian manuals, who was also a distinguished soldier, philosopher and agriculturist, was familiar with the existence of a curb bit, although he never employed one. He used the snaffle, terming it either 'smooth' or 'rough' according to the shape of the *icheni* (literally 'seahorses') that were built into or round the mouthpiece. *Icheni* were

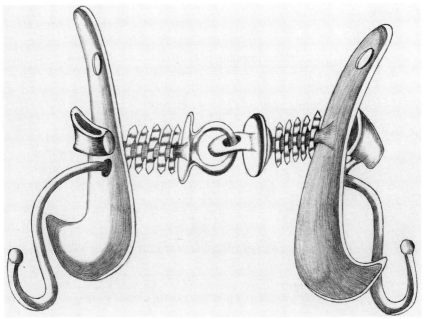

A Greek bit of about the fourth century BC fitted with *icheni* which would, one imagines, have caused Xenophon to describe the mouthpiece as being 'rough'

rollers encircling the mouthpiece, the spikes of which were either short and blunt or sharper and longer.

Xenophon wrote: 'It is not the bit but its use that results in a horse showing its pleasure so that it yields to the hand; there is no need for harsh measures; he should rather be coaxed on so that he will go forward most cheerfully in his swift paces.'

He recommended the use of soft bits and emphasised the need for lightness in the rider's hand. Use, however, was made of the *psalion*, a metal cavesson acting on the nose, which was the precursor of the Iberian *careta* and the *caveçon* of the Renaissance horsemen.

What is surprising is that since then *no* major innovations and *no* advances of any significance have been made in the systems of bitting and these are, if anything, even less well understood today than two thousand years ago. In fact, there has been only one attempt to create 'a new concept in bitting' that would eradicate the imprecision of the imperfect conventional bit. Unhappily, it failed in a constructional detail and was withdrawn from the market on that account. (The Wellep bit is discussed later.)

The Assyrians

Although Xenophon's treatises on management, training and riding provide a clear insight into his deep understanding of the bit's role as a part of a system of equitation, it was a system that could place no reliance on a saddle for the security of the rider's seat. It is the detailed Assyrian artefacts to which, very largely, we must turn for visual evidence. The Assyrians were a world power three centuries before the birth of Xenophon. Initially they were

The ornate and sophisticated Assyrian bridle. It is possible that it was used with the addition of a noseband attached to the bit

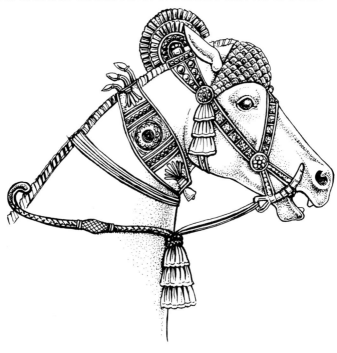

a chariot people and early depictions of Assyrians riding horses show them sitting apprehensively, gripping with the calves and being led by attendants. By the reign of Tiglath-Pileser III (747–727 BC), the Assyrian armoured cavalry presents a totally different picture. Now we see confident riders, spearmen and archers, on spirited, immaculately coiffured horses, all stallions, of course, which they ride in ornate bridles that are sophisticated by any standard. The jointed snaffle bit has a cheek shaped like an inverted Y. It has been suggested that bits of this type were originally made from antler-tine and that later patterns, made of metal, followed the antler design. There are, indeed, some examples of Assyrian bits in which the cheeks are fashioned in an animal motif, most noticeably models of reindeer! Both types are found not only in the regions in which the Assyrians operated, but throughout the Caucasus, modern Iran and central Asia – a fact that adds strength to the hypothesis of the reindeer as the forerunner of subsequent horse cultures.

It appears that the Assyrian bits, in particular those fitted to chariot horses, may sometimes have been used in conjunction with a noseband fastened under the bit or attached to the bit itself. The addition of a noseband would obviously add to the strength of the bit. Nosebands of this sort, which we know as drop-nosebands, made their appearance early in recorded history. A relief on the tomb of Horenhab of Egypt, one of the first records of a man sitting on an obviously spirited mount, shows a horse with just such a noseband. It is dated to about 1600 BC and the rider sits on his horse's rump, as men of his time and previously would have sat on an ass, and as men in the Middle East still ride their donkeys today.

As horses became bigger, as a result, in part, of selective breding, but particularly because of the greater availability of cereals, which gave a higher protein diet, so the means of control had, of necessity, to be made more effective and therefore more severe. The niceties of riding from leg into hand would not have entered the philosophy of these pre-Christian horsemen who marched and fought with no more than a saddle-cloth between them and their horses, as mounted warriors were to do for almost the next thousand years.

Xenophon, it is true, advocated the use of smooth bits as

being more effective on the trained horse than the rough ones fitted with spikes and so on. He also appreciated the value of mouthpieces fitted with rollers or short lengths of chain that would encourage the horse to 'mouth' the bit – he talks of the horse 'pursuing the bit' with its tongue. The object, of course, is to encourage the relaxation of the lower jaw, and those bits fitted with 'keys' that we use today on young horses for the same purpose would not have been unfamiliar to the horsemen of Ancient Greece.

It was to be a long time, however, before the world began to think in such terms. The nomadic, steppe horsemen of central Asia were the exception to the general rule, always riding in light simple snaffle bits, although they rode by instinct, without bothering their heads too much about the science of the thing.

The Persian Horsemen

From the demise of the Assyrian Empire and its replacement as the superpower of antiquity by the Persians in the sixth century BC, horsemen became increasingly preoccupied with forceful bitting arrangements, using mechanical restraints to achieve control. (Right up to Caprilli's time at Tor di Quinto and Pinerolo at the end of the nineteenth century, the curb bit dominated equestrian thought and practice in Europe and it is only in the last half-century that the snaffle has assumed a universal ascendancy.)

By the third century BC, the Persian Empire stretched from Egypt to Asia Minor and from India to the Greek islands. To a very large extent its supremacy was underpinned by Persian possession of the powerful Nisean horse. Bigger and stronger than those used by previous peoples, it was an object of admiration in the ancient world. As well as being heavier, it was also a coarser, less refined specimen in comparison with the horses that had carried the Assyrians and Babylonians on their conquests, but it was hard and very strong. It was the result of cross-breeding over a period of 1,500 years, and without much doubt it included infusions of the Mongolian wild horse, as Persian influence extended into Mongolia.

Herodotus, describing the armies of Cyrus the Great, wrote:

'The armoured Persian horsemen and the death-dealing chariots were invincible, no man dared face them ...'. Invincible they may have been, but the strong, spirited, heavily crested stallions, well fed and conditioned, posed problems for horsemen with no more than a padded cloth to sit on. It was easier for the chariot driver, who could brace himself against the front board of the vehicle and put his weight on the reins, but the rider had no such advantage and had also to carry his weapons.

Persian reliefs show these thick-necked horses in what we would term an overbent position, with chin tucked in against the chest. It is possible, and has been suggested by eminent authorities, that the nosebands worn by the horses, which are quite clearly visible, could have incorporated spikes or burrs on the inside surface on the principle of the Spanish *careta*. This would account for the head position, particularly as the noseband appears to be attached to the bit itself.

The Persians may have copied this device from the Indians with whom they had close contacts. It was certainly in use in India in the first century and one has to suppose that it could have been about for a long time before that. Conversely, of course, the Indians might have borrowed it from the Persians, but what is certain is that the latter were among the first to use a noseband of that type. The *careta* survived into the Moorish horse culture to become a part of the Iberian system and the inspiration for the Western hackamore, being taken to the Americas by the sixteenth-century *conquistadores*. It was evident in the Renaissance schools of 'classical' horsemanship and was certainly the base for the *caveçon*, a piece of equipment in general use throughout Europe, which had its origins in the Iberian Peninsula.

Indeed, this is the first time in history that horses are depicted in an overbent position. The Assyrian horses are always shown with legs extended to front and rear and, despite their arched crests, with the face well in advance of the vertical. The Greek horses often carry the head close to the horizontal plane, but with the hindlegs well engaged beneath the body. Both postures are understandable when one takes into account the upward-lifting action of the snaffle and, additionally, the absence of a saddle. Without a saddle, even the best of horsemen might rely to some degree upon the reins for their security.

The Persian bridle

The Persian bridle is notable as it set a pattern for those of the following centuries and it is still echoed today in the bridles of the Argentine *gaucho* and the Ukrainian Cossack.

Its points of attachment to the bit were made with toggles, in the absence of buckles, and it often employed straps that crossed the face diagonally (like the *gaucho* bridle). For some strange reason, straps across the face, or one running up centrally from both rings of the bit, like the Australian cheeker on the racecourse, provide a psychological restraint, causing the horse to hold back rather than pull into the device.

The bridle cheek-pieces divided to fasten onto a phallus-shaped bit cheek that was often decorated at the lower end with the shape of a horse's hoof. Both features are symbolic of the stallion's fertility and the design persists in the present-day 'horseshoe-cheek' stallion bits. Pressure on the bit rein tightened the spike noseband by virtue of the noseband's direct connection with the bit. A degree of poll pressure would also have been exerted by a bit of this shape, although not as much as can be obtained with a curb bit. Pressure on the poll induces a lowering of the head and thus contributes to the control obtainable.

The Middle Ages

The invention of the curb bit, adapted by North African horsemen to become the notorious ring bit used by the Nobades, a negroid race employed by the Romans as cavalry *foederati*, and then by the Mamelukes, began a system of control, via pressures applied on the lever principle, of enormous and, indeed, jaw-breaking potential. The ring bit is still in use in North Africa, but the excessively severe curb bit of the Middle Ages, its mouthpiece made more horrendous by high ports, spikes and rollers, and with cheeks up to 55 cm (22 in) in length, has now been consigned to the museums.

Allowing for the heavy, less responsive type of horse that was

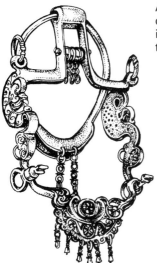

A North African ring bit, sometimes called the Mameluke. Surprisingly, it is still to be found in North Africa to this day

developed to carry a heavily armoured man as well as its own protective clothing, the use of such fearsome curb bits none the less implies a high degree of skill. There is no doubt that the medieval knight had learnt how to control the horse with leg and spur. The bit was operated with one hand only, the left hand. This held the rein and also the shield and had therefore to be carried chest high, while the right hand bore the sword, lance or mace.

Whether 'in press of battle' the mounted knight of the Middle Ages practised the rears, leaps and kicks comprising the classical 'airs above the ground' is sometimes disputed. However, there is no reason to suppose that the horses were not trained to kick out behind to discourage infantry attempting to take them from the rear. A *levade* (half-rear) would certainly be a deterrent to foot soldiers and if the horse were to leap forward in something resembling a *capriole*, that would have had a most salutary effect.

A pirouette or half-pirouette would have been a necessary accomplishment, allowing all-round use of the sword arm. Indeed, there is ample evidence to show that the horses, until they became impossibly overburdened and heavy, were handy and much attention was paid to the schooling of what were considered animals of great value. They would certainly have responded to a neck rein, while the raised bridle hand, threatening a more coercive action when used with a bit of the dimensions described, was possibly quite sufficient to keep the horse under restraint. The Californian rider today does the same thing with the 'spade' bit, the nearest modern equivalent to the medieval curb, having first schooled the horse in a succession of nosebands. As the horse becomes more obedient and balanced, lighter nosebands are used until, in the end, control passes to the bit which, though potentially severe, need not be handled other than with the lightest of hands.

This method of 'mouthing' the horse through its nose was inherent in Moorish horsemanship throughout the Moorish occupation of the Iberian Peninsula and it is impossible to imagine that it was not borrowed, in part, by European horsemen.

The Classical Masters

The masters of the classical Renaissance schools of Naples inherited the traditions of Byzantine horsemanship, a riding school being founded there by a Byzantine group in 1134, which based its teaching on the Byzantine Circus. When the first of the classical Renaissance masters, Federico Grisone, founded his school in Naples in 1532, his teaching was derived from Xenophon, certainly, but also from the Byzantine tradition, which had an inevitable influence on the horsemanship of the Middle Ages.

Grisone, and many of those who followed him, used some very severe curb bits, many of the more complex ones being designed by Grisone himself, and they practised methods that the twentieth century would condemn as being cruel beyond belief. The emphasis was upon continual 'correction' with brief moments of 'cherishing'. In fact, the reward amounted to not much more than a cessation of punishment – but then this was also the age of the rack and the thumb screw, when heretics were flayed alive or, more mercifully, burnt at the stake.

None the less, Grisone insisted upon preserving the lightness

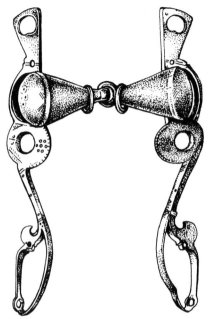

'Cannon bit' of the sixteenth century which had the advantage of a broad mouthpiece if nothing else

and sensitivity of the mouth in a manner that would be quite foreign to the modern rider brought up on the philosophy of constant (and sometimes twang-taut) contact. Grisone, of course, also wanted contact, but preferably by the *weight of the rein*. This is the difference separating the art form represented by the classical school from modern dressage riding, which is more nearly a sport than an art. The masters of the seventeenth and eighteenth centuries preserved as an ideal (virtually the Holy Grail of the equestrian art) an extreme lightness of hand, performing the most advanced movements on a gently looping rein.

This remained an inherent tenet of the Iberian school in Spain and Portugal, the cradles of the classic art, and is still to be seen there. The late Maestro Nuno Oliveira was a supreme exponent of school riding practised as an art and spectacle for its own sake and even today there are Spanish and Portuguese horsemen who increase the strength of the bit by adding an inch-long piece of silver onto the light, rolled leather

The early Masters made much use of the 'false' rein attached to the cavesson rings. The bit rein, despite the potential severity of the bit, was held in a gentle loop. (*Capriole* by Baron Reis d'Eisenberg – eighteenth century.)

rein to give it more weight! If confronted by a horse ridden with such light contact, present-day dressage judges would condemn the animal as being 'behind the bit' or not being 'on the bit'. (What, one wonders, would have been the modern reaction to that most loyal Ecuyer of Versailles, the Marquis de la Bigne, one of the most distinguished of the eminent masters of the *ancien régime*. For a wager, he rode his horse at a very slow, unbroken canter across the courtyard fronting the Palace of Versailles, on the proverbial silk thread!)

Grisone and the classical masters, up to the master of them all, François Robichon de la Guérinière, employed the *caveçon*

Caprioles à Droite.

Igr. le Marg.

A horse in an advanced stage of training being schooled by the Duke of Newcastle in the *capriole*. The rider is using the curb directly but the rein is held lightly in the classic loop

in ridden school work, an item almost exactly similar to the lunge cavesson of today. The word *caveçon* is applied to a halter worn in military fashion under the bridle but, of course, it has its origins as a controlling or schooling aid in the *careta* and in those studded nosebands of antiquity. In its more severe forms it was no more than an instrument of torture. Thomas Blundeville (1565) wrote of English riders employing a chain noseband (directly derived from the Moorish practice but much heavier and, it seems, used less sympathetically) that he considered to be too severe 'for that it straineth the tender gristle of his nose too sore'. The *musrole*, made of twisted iron, was a similar device and was also condemned by Grisone as being counter-productive, causing the nose 'by its violence ... to arise in the middle like the beak of a hawk'.

The curb bit, usually with a high port allowing direct pressure on the bars and yet often fitted with 'keys', was used initially with a cavesson to which was secured the 'false rein'. The bit rein was held loosely, no use being made of it, and the horse ridden through the pressure on its nose.

Later, the rein was transferred to the 'flying trench', an addition attached above the bit's mouthpiece that was the forerunner of the bradoon now employed in a double bridle. If the 'flying trench' was not used, then the top (bradoon) rein was fastened to the top ring of the curb in the fashion that has become known as a Pelham.

The curb, therefore, was never brought into full play, the horse being ridden on the top or 'false rein' and by the *threat* of the bit's potentially severe action.

The schooling was, of course, dependent upon a mechanical force applied directly by the cavesson and 'false rein' and then, secondarily, by the threat of the powerful curb. From contemporary writings it is clear that the horses suffered severe galling and callousing on the nose. However, it must be remembered that the horses of Grisone's time were common, heavy leftovers from a previous era, bred to carry an armoured knight. To make it possible for these ungainly creatures to perform the balanced and highly collected paces of the *manège*, let alone the 'airs above the ground', that are the manifestation of ultimate collection, it was necessary to engage the hindlegs deep under the body, involving a significant lowering of the quarters and a corresponding lightening and raising of the forehand. The horse, without doubt, was *pulled* into this shortened form from one end and to some degree *pushed* in at the other by the whip and spur, the whip frequently being applied below the hocks by an assistant on the ground. Two hundred years later, when the horses were lighter and more responsive, the coercive school had given way to the concept of riding as a rational science and as an art form, and was exemplified as such by Guérinière. None the less, the demands of collection, and the absence in Europe of any necessity to leave the ground in order to jump over obstacles, ensured that the accent lay firmly on the curb bit, a preoccupation that extended well into the nineteenth century. Even in hunting England, where collection in European terms was an unwanted quality in the galloping, high-couraged 'blood' horse that crossed the strongly fenced Shire countries so well, the curb bit and then the double bridle were *de rigeur* and were to remain so almost up to the Second World War.

The Nineteenth Century

'There are', it used to be said by the hunting die-hards, 'three kinds of fool. The fool, the bloody fool and the man who hunts in a snaffle.' (Writing nearly 30 years ago, I was bold enough to expand the trio of stupidity into a quartet. 'There is', I wrote, 'one more. The fool who believes this!')

Loriners' catalogues of the nineteenth century reflect the preoccupation faithfully, particularly, perhaps, that of Benjamin Latchford, who carried on his business as a loriner (i.e. a maker of bits, spurs and stirrup irons) at 11 Upper St Martin's Lane, London. Latchford published *The Loriner – Opinions and Observations on Bridle-Bits and the Suitable Bitting of Horses* in 1883 and included 'A Treatise on the Suitable Bitting of Horses' by the Spanish authority of the day, Don Juan Segundo, which had been written in 1832. In this work, Segundo recommended a complex system of bridles, based on the conformation of the mouth, that involved interchangeable cheeks (then called 'branches'), mouthpieces and curb chains. He claimed that every sort of equine vice or virtue could be catered for by a correct choice of the different parts. It was an ingenious system, based on sound 'mechanical' principles and had some success in Europe without finding favour in the English market, even though Latchford claims to have had a good demand for the bits.

Latchford, who was to achieve immortality with the sentence, 'There is a key to every horse's mouth', illustrated a wide range of bits, many of them complex and all beautifully crafted in hand-forged steel. Interestingly, he stated that the bit that suited more horses than any other was his Melton Mouth, a simple thick-mouthed curb and bradon with a fairly shallow port that

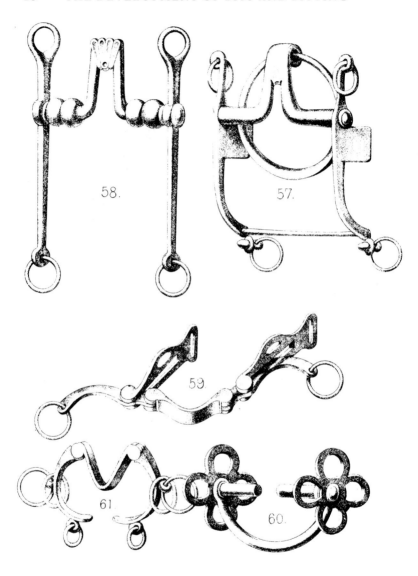

A page from *The Loriner*, Benjamin Latchford's treatise on bridle bits published in 1883. These bits, including the fearsome ring bit (Item 57), were in use at that time. Item 59 is an interesting nose bridle on the pattern of the Renaissance cavesson

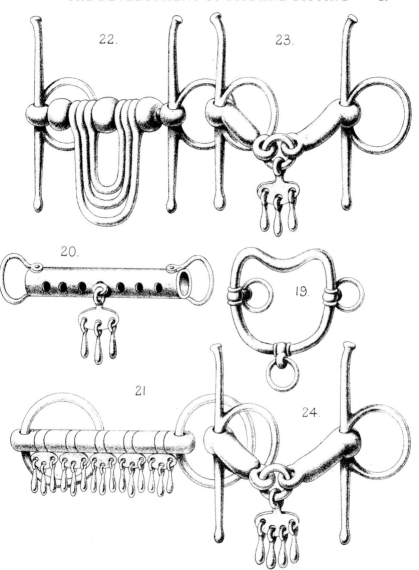

A selection of breaking and training bits from *The Loriner*. Item 22 has a tongue grid to prevent that organ from being put over the bit's mouthpiece. Item 20 is really a 'flute' bit. The perforated mouth frustrates the inhalation of air made by a 'windsucker'. Item 19 is Chifney's lead and anti-rear bit for yearlings would not be out of place today. But then Latchford also wrote 'of every twenty bits I make, nineteen are for men's heads and not more than one really for the horse's head'. That piece of good sense is, alas, not nearly so often quoted.

(Latchford worked closely with a Frenchman, Chevasse, who settled in Walsall in about 1896, carrying on the predominantly French influence in the craft of lorinery that had begun following the Norman invasion of Britain in 1066. The early Ordinances of the Loriners, one of the most ancient of the City Companies, dated 1245 during the reign of Henry III, is signed by 'Wardens of the Mystery', all of whom bear Norman French names.)

Federico Caprilli

The Caprilli revolution that stood accepted theory and practice on their heads, discarded 'school riding' and collection for a 'natural', forward system in which there was no place for a curb bit and in which the hand, attached to a snaffle bit, was always a 'forward' hand, never the retracting hand that was more often than not a feature of school riding in the cavalry establishments of the period. (Caprilli taught at the Italian cavalry schools at Tor di Quinto and Pinerolo between 1894 and 1907. In that year he died in Turin after fainting while riding his horse at walk. See 'Caprilli the Innovator' in the companion book in this series *The Saddle – A Guide to Fitting and Purpose*.)

'The difference between natural riding and dressage', wrote Caprilli in one of his rare, execrably handwritten notes, 'is that this one [i.e. dressage] strives to adapt the horse to the rider, while the other adapts the rider to the horse.' (To 'adapt the horse to the rider' involves, to a very large extent, reliance upon the mechanical action of the bit and an emphasis upon the retreating hand, both of which were anathema to those who promoted Caprillist principles.) Of the bit he wrote, 'For my part I always found that horses go much better in a snaffle,' and he never deviated in his adherence to the snaffle as being central to *il sistema*.

However, despite the adoption, either wholly or in part, of Caprillist principles, including the use of the snaffle by the greatest of the showjumping riders in the period between the two world wars, such as Jack Talbot-Ponsonby and Joe Hume-Dudgeon, the snaffle had by no means acquired the universal recognition it enjoys today. Saddlers' catalogues of this time are full of every sort of 'novelty' bit, many of them Pelhams of one sort or another, all claiming to improve the rider's control and the carriage of the horse. The variety available was enormous and, by present-day standards, economically impossible; a great many bits were hand-forged and it was possible to have one-off bits made to order.

It was a situation that revealed all too clearly the continuing obsession with mechanical exactitude and the control and positioning of the head by those same means that had so occupied the minds of the horsemen of antiquity. In hindsight, the concern was overwhelmingly with the control of the horse and the imposition of an overall outline or posture through the hand. The idea of riding the horse from the back to the front, i.e. from the leg into the hand, was not really much in evidence. (This process was best described when my very distinguished French instructor exhorted me always to ride the horse 'arseways, frontwards, forward'. I have never forgotten it and commend the instruction wholeheartedly.)

Even very expert horsemen, who had been trained at Weedon cavalry school, particularly, perhaps, if they were polo enthusiasts, shared the preoccupation with the bit, if not as the panacea of all equine ills then at least as a major factor in the

The fitting of a Rugby Pelham

MILLER'S LIFETIME NEVER-RUST PELHAM BITS

No. 1700 — LIFETIME NEVER-RUST MULLEN MOUTH PELHAM BIT: Loose cheeks from 4½" to 7". With curb chain and hooks. Price...**$4.95**

No. 1705 — As above but with oversize 5¼" or 5½" mouth. 6" or 7" cheeks. With curb chain and hooks. Price...**$5.75**

No. 1710 — LIGHT-WEIGHT MULLEN MOUTH PELHAM BIT: As our No. 1700 but in a utility weight for riding schools. Never-Rust. With curb chain and hooks. Price...**$3.50**

No. 1712 — PONY MULLEN PELHAM BIT: As No. 1710 but in pony size. With curb chain and hooks. Price...**$3.25**

No. 1714—STAR STEEL SILVER MULLEN MOUTH PELHAM BIT: 5" mouth, 7" loose cheeks. With curb chain and hooks.
Price...8/16" heft **$6.50**
Price...9/16" heft **$7.25**

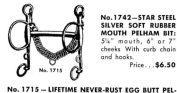
No. 1715

No. 1715 — LIFETIME NEVER-RUST EGG BUTT PELHAM BIT: 5" mouth. Cheeks from 4½" to 7". With curb chain and hooks. Price...**$5.50**

No. 1717—As above but with 5¼" or 5½" mouth. 6" or 7" cheeks. With curb chain and hooks. Price...**$5.95**

•

Lifetime Never-Rust bits are cast of metal that has a brilliant lustre. Guaranteed for life against breakage.

No. 1720 — LIFETIME NEVER-RUST LOOSE RING PELHAM BIT: 5" mouth. 6", 6½" and 7" stiff cheeks. With curb chain and hooks. Price...**$4.50**

No.1725—STAR STEEL SILVER LOOSE RING PELHAM BIT: 5" mouth, 7" cheeks. With curb chain and hooks. Price...**$6.25**

No. 1740 — LIFETIME NEVER-RUST SOFT RUBBER MOUTH PELHAM BIT: Popular for tender mouths. Has a strong welded chain under the soft rubber mouthpiece. 5¼" mouth. Cheeks from 6" to 7". With curb chain and hooks. Price...**$6.75**

No.1742—STAR STEEL SILVER SOFT RUBBER MOUTH PELHAM BIT: 5¼" mouth, 6" or 7" cheeks. With curb chain and hooks. Price...**$6.50**

No. 1730 — LIFETIME NEVER-RUST HARD RUBBER MOUTH PELHAM BIT: This famous bit has hard rubber permanently molded to mouthpiece. A concealed metal collar at sides of mouth adds greater strength. Cheeks from 4" to 7". With curb chain and hooks. Price...**$6.95**

No. 1735 — PONY HARD RUBBER MOUTH BIT: As above but in pony size. With curb chain and hooks. Price...**$6.75**

No. 1745 — LIFETIME NEVER-RUST HARD RUBBER MOUTH NINTH LANCERS PELHAM BIT: Has three loops for curb rein. Hard rubber mouth has concealed metal collar at each end. 5" mouth, 7½" flat cheeks. With curb chain and hooks. Price...**$8.75**

No.1750—STAR STEEL SILVER TOM THUMB PELHAM BIT: Has 3⅞" loose sliding cheeks. 4¾" mouth. With curb chain and hooks. Price...**$6.25**

No. 1755 — LIFETIME NEVER-RUST HART-WELL PELHAM BIT: 5" mouth. 6", 6½" and 7" loose cheeks. With curb chain and hooks. Price...**$6.25**

No. 1760 — As above but with 5¼" or 5½" mouth. With curb chain and hooks. **$6.75**

No.1765—STAR STEEL SILVER HARTWELL PELHAM BIT: 4¾" mouth, 5½" cheeks. With curb chain and hooks. Price...**$7.25**

No. 1770 — LIFETIME NEVER-RUST RUGBY PELHAM BIT: Has solid cheeks, flat rings. 5" mouth. 5½" to 7" cheeks. With curb chain and hooks. Price...**$7.50**

No.1775—STAR STEEL SILVER RUGBY PELHAM BIT: 5" mouth, 6" cheeks. With curb chain and hooks. Price...**$9.75**

No. 1780 — LIFETIME NEVER-RUST JOINTED MOUTH PELHAM BIT: Cheeks from 5½" to 7". With curb chain and hooks. Price...**$4.75**

No. 1785 — STAR STEEL SILVER JOINTED MOUTH PELHAM BIT: Has 6½" loose cheeks, 5½" mouth. With curb chain and hooks. Price...**$7.95**

A group of Pelham bits taken from an American catalogue of the 1950s when bits of this pattern formed a substantial part of the overall sales. The Rugby Pelham is numbered 1770. It is probably the most satisfactory of the group

BITS

EGG-LINK PELHAM   VULCANITE PORT PELHAM   HOLLOW MOUTH PELHAM

HOLLOW MOUTH

184 Wood Mouth

DEWSBURY
Trade Mark

BREAKING BIT 12/6

FAUDEL PHILLIPS'S FLAT MOUTH PELHAM

HUNTING SNAFFLE   DEE RACE SNAFFLE

2537
"Jodphur"
Curb,
Flat
Links   DEWSBURY
Trade Mark

ANTI-REARING BIT

"DOUBLE SNAPS", 12/6.

A page from a pre-War catalogue issued by the English firm Distas. It shows the interesting flat-mouth Pelham and the 'Jodphur' polo curb. The shaping of the snaffle mouthpieces allows the bit to conform more easily to the mouth. In this respect snaffles of that time were much superior to those obtainable today horse's carriage, obedience, handiness and way of going. Moreover, they approached the subject scientifically, calculating the exact relationship between the length of the cheek above and below the mouthpiece in relationship to the width of the bit, and studying every tiny detail of fitting in relation to the conformation of the mouth and tongue.

Major-General Geoffrey Brooke, a member of the British jumping team in the mid-1920s, a top-class polo player and a horseman of international repute, summed it up in a foreword he contributed to Cecil G. Trew's *The Accoutrements of the Riding Horse*. He wrote:

> Today we come across what can best be described as a fancy bit for some exceptional purpose, designed by some enthusiast who is convinced that he has achieved the alpha and omega of horse control. In the past similar attempts were made to solve similar problems that confronted horsemen of those days.
>
> In this respect I myself am a culprit: once possessing a pony whose mouth became dry and lost its sensitiveness, I had a bit forged, by either Messrs. Whippy or Sowter [leading saddlers of the day], which consisted of two hollow cylindrical bars, the smaller one screwed into the larger. Each was perforated on one side and the inner filled with sweet oil. When the bit was turned slightly over, the oil flowed from the inner into the outer cylinder and dripped on the animal's tongue. I admit it was not a widespread success.

The same epitaph could be applied to a hundred more of those pre-war oddities.

Sheer economic pressure in the period after the Second World War put an end to all that. The last hand-forger in Walsall put up the shutters in the 1960s and the horse world learnt (probably to the relief of all horses) how to manage with a greatly reduced range of production-line bits.

Up to the 1960s, the Midlands town of Walsall was the world's largest producer of horse-furniture and general lorinery, supplying even the exotic demands of the South American market. Drop-forged stainless steel was available and so were some very excellent alloys, like Eglantine and Kangaroo, as well, of course, as the cheap and notoriously unreliable solid nickel.

For the most part, the Walsall bits were not only very well made but also retained the shaping of the mouthpiece and the cheeks that had proved so satisfactory in the past.

Economics, combined with outdated production systems, destroyed the Walsall output in a matter of a few years and at the end of the 1960s the bit manufacturing trade had passed very largely to the Far East. In time, the finish became as good as that of Walsall, but the detail of design (in relation to the horse's mouth) deteriorated significantly. Today, Germany has a thriving lorinery industry, producing items of excellent quality, and Walsall, although no longer the leader in the field, is still responsible for some of the best lorinery in the world.

Bit sizes are now standardised and bespoke bits, made to 1·5 mm (¹⁄₁₆ in), in terms of mouth size and diameter of the mouthpiece, are now heirlooms. The gimmicks have gone and the horse world of the 1990s relies upon the snaffle.

If we have lost anything, it is that we no longer pay attention to the finer details of bitting. There is no awareness of the importance of fitting exactly the correct mouthpiece that will conform to the mouth of the individual horse and very few modern horsemen and women have anything but the most superficial knowledge of a subject that, like the fitting of the saddle, contributes so much to the horse's comfort and performance level. Possibly as a result, we now hear very much about contact and very, very little about the importance of the 'good hands' that were the hallmark of the best of the pre-war riders and were, for every pre-war Pony Club child, the 'consummation devoutly to be wished' and pursued.

The New Riders

The post-war period was marked by a remarkable increase in the numbers of people riding and owning horses. Many of these new owners, some of whom, in time, would inevitably become the instructors and leaders of the new horse world, did not come from the traditional country background that had dominated British riding between the wars. Their homes were on the outskirts of the towns and cities in which most of them earned their living. Some followed the traditional British horse activity of hunting, but for most hunting was not the principal motivation for horse-keeping and quite quickly the emphasis in British riding passed from the hunting field to competitive riding, which had the advantage of going on throughout the year and fitted more conveniently into the lifestyle of riders who had homes to run and jobs to hold down. Much of this widespread activity was made possible by the growth of the Riding Club movement, the clubs holding regular instructional rallies, and so on. Interest in schooling on the flat, in accordance with a systematic programme of training – which, though well understood in Europe, was no more than a minority interest in Britain at the end of the Second World War – increased quickly, for the new riders were probably more receptive and enquiring than their predecessors, brought up in the shadow of the hunting field.

A handful of very good riding instructors, were becoming established in Britain – men and women who had either been influenced by the European schools or were products of them. Jack Hance was still teaching; Joe Hume-Dudgeon had his school in Dublin and Tony Collings was at Porlock. There were the Sheddens, Paddy Burke, Jack Talbot-Ponsonby, Brian Young, Robert Hall, the controversial Charles Harris and a few more, including Edy Goldman, considered by many to be the best teacher of them all.

As a better understanding of basic schooling became more established, so the bitting arrangements became increasingly simple. The complex mouthpieces and attachments, now, in any event, uneconomical to manufacture, began to be consigned to the recesses of the saddler's shop, their place being taken by the snaffle. At one time the most common forms were the cheek snaffle, which became known as the Fulmer, and the so-called German snaffle, which featured a thick, broad mouthpiece. Both were used, more often than not, with a drop noseband, an article rarely seen in Britain between the wars but commonplace in Europe where it was considered to be an integral part of the bridle.

(This certainly did not happen overnight, of course. As late as

1969 I took a course for young people in North Wales, one that I held annually for a number of years. On the first day of instruction I was dumbfounded to see the range of horrendous bitting arrangements that came before me. Taking my courage in both hands I ordered the removal of every martingale and every bit other than a plain snaffle. Parents were convinced that their ewe lambs would be carried off into the distant mountains and never seen again, and they said so forcefully. I remained adamant and within 24 hours the ponies, far from taking off, had settled, with, one imagines, sighs of heartfelt relief, to working in something approaching an acceptable shape.)

Riding techniques improved dramatically, and they continue to do so. Performances followed suit, assisted by courses that, whether for showjumping or cross-country trials, were designed expertly, scientifically and with no little artistry.

What has not improved – and one has only to peruse the BHS examination syllabi for proof – is an understanding of the principles involved in the construction and fitting of saddles and the bitting of the horse. The importance and relevance of both were better appreciated and more closely studied a century ago, even though equitational theory had yet to develop to accord with our thinking, and despite the 'mechanical' approach that was to pertain nearly to the present time. For that reason, we need to be able to place the bit in perspective, within the combination of aids used by the rider, and, of course, in relation to the mouth to which it is fitted.

2: The Role of the Bit

It is all too easy for the bit to be viewed in isolation and used as a means of correcting shortcomings caused by inadequate schooling or the inexperience of the rider. In actual fact, of course, when applied in that way the bit causes more problems than it ever cures.

For the bit to be put in its proper perspective, it has to be looked at as part of the *combination of natural aids* and viewed, therefore, with some understanding of the equitational theory involved, from which it cannot be separated. Quite obviously, unless riders understand the theory, they can hardly be expected to put it into practice.

In essence, the bit is no more than an extension of the hand aid, the two being joined by a rein. That remains true whatever form the bit may take, even though the action will vary according to its shape and the position it occupies in the mouth. Ideally, the bit should be seen as the last link in the chain of natural aids. It follows the action of the legs to conform with the basic principle of riding the horse from the back to the front, in fact from the legs into the hands (or, in the already quoted instruction of my French instructor, 'Arseways, frontwards, forwards').

It is at this very elementary point that the problems arise. They do so because most people do exactly the opposite – they ride from *front to back*, relying on the bit to correct deviations in the direction of travel and, more often than not, attempting to use it to alter the position of the head. They do so because the myth of the divine right of the Anglo-Saxon in respect of all things horsy still persists. We do not play a piano or a violin by instinct, nor for that matter do we drive cars without some initial instruction. Why, therefore, should it be thought that we do not need to learn how to ride a horse other than by practise?

By the time a great many would-be riders reach a competent instructor, they are already pretty well confirmed in the habit of riding from the front end with a retreating hand. Long ago when rough-riding sergeant-instructors took a new squad into the riding school for the first time, they would ask the question, ''Ow many of you genelmen 'ave learnt to ride?' This was followed immediately by the instruction, 'One step forward march!' Only the excessively and unwisely enthusiastic moved a muscle. Those who stepped forward, confident in their ability 'to 'witch the world with noble horsemanship', were at once brought firmly down to earth. 'Right, genelmen! This is were we begin to *un*learn yer!' And they did. That is the problem for most instructors. They have to undo, in a relatively short time, faults acquired over years.

Until we ride from back to front, letting our legs, which control the quarters, dominate the directional changes and correct unwanted movements, while also initiating, with the help of the upper body, the changes in outline, the gaits of the horse are unnecessarily restricted, even to the point of becoming unlevel, and the flexion of the joints is limited. The whole business of effective locomotion, of free, forward movement, is at once put at risk and all because of the overriding influence of the hand and its extension, the bit. (These faults in the movement, caused by the inexpert or *unthinking* use of the hand, can very quickly become habitual. It is then very difficult and time-consuming to 'free' the horse so that whatever potential does exist can be realised.)

My favourite teaching diagram (see overleaf) illustrates the aid combination and is called the Wheel of Equitation: it is rather like the Buddhist's Wheel of Life in which all things strive to be in harmony. My wheel is simpler, however, in that it comprises no more than a hub and four spokes.

The hub is the rider's seat, secure, in balance and independent, so far as that is humanly possible (and acquired, for preference, through painstaking work on the lunge with a good instructor).

The four spokes are: the *head* (thought before action – how often do we see a performance fail on this account?); the *trunk* and *body weight*; the *legs*; the *hands*.

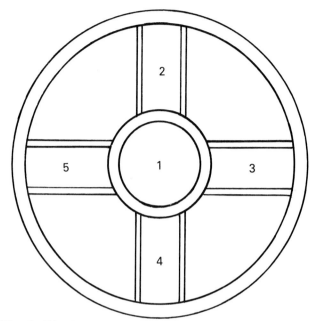

The Wheel of Equitation – 'rather like the Buddhist's Wheel of Life in which all things strive to be in harmony': 1 = the seat; 2 = the head; 3 = the trunk and body weight; 4 = the legs; 5 = the hands

All are interdependent. If the legs cannot be used effectively and in conjunction with each other; or if the rider is stiff and unyielding in the upper body, and thus unable to conform to the movement of the horse, then the spoke that these parts represent within the Wheel loses strength and is reduced in its function. In consequence of support to the rim being reduced or removed, the Wheel buckles and is in danger of collapse.

The Wheel's construction depends upon the hub – take it away and you have no wheel at all.

What emerges is that the bit, whatever form it may take, becomes more or less effective according to the ability of the rider and the horse's level of training.

The whole matter can be summarised, and the answer found

to a legion of queries ending in 'What bit should I use?', in just three words: *learn to ride.*

The Object of the Bit

In basic terms, it could be said that the object of the bit is that, when used in conjunction with the remaining aids, it combines the functions of the steering wheel (in part) and brake. It is, therefore, implicit to control. That admittedly incomplete definition is probably the one generally held. It is, however, capable of being extended.

The bit, whatever its shape, acts primarily to govern the impulsion created by the legs and seat, which, in itself, will involve a greater engagement of the hindlegs and maximum flexion of their joints. The bit contains the energy thus created, or releases it to the degree required, so shortening or lengthening the outline.

Furthermore, it channels the direction of the forward thrust produced by the quarters when applied in one or other of the five rein effects.

Its effect becomes more or less efficient according to the energy (impulsion) created. Without impulsion the horse becomes like a boat that is becalmed; the loss of wind in the sail and the absence of forward movement makes any action of the rudder meaningless.

On that basis the action of the bit can be defined as follows:

1 It assists changes of direction, either from the straight line to one hand or the other, or when moving the horse laterally. It does so when applied in conjunction with the leg and the altered body weight.
2 It acts to regulate the gait and effect transitions from one to another when applied *following* the action of the legs.*
3 It acts with the body and leg aids to produce alterations in the outline, i.e. a shortening or lengthening of the horse's base.

---

*Although the leg action precedes that of the hand, the degree by which it does so is often so minimal as to be almost simultaneous.

To understand the place of the bit in the combination of aids and then use it efficiently, one has to appreciate that the head and neck move independently of the rest of the body. They do not dictate the position of the shoulders, which, conversely, are directly connected to the quarters in which the directional movement originates. Where the quarters point, there the horse must go.

Changes of direction are first prepared for by positioning the haunches and are then executed with the head (in response to the bit action) leading the movement.

Directional Changes and the Five Rein Effects

I imagine that nine riders out of ten execute a turn by acting with the inside hand in the third rein effect, i.e. the direct rein of opposition, and I suspect a similar number do so without ever having heard of rein effects, much less of reins of opposition.

The five rein effects are simple enough to understand, although it is somewhat more difficult to acquire the knack of using them to best advantage. However, there is no denying that they contribute substantially to the armoury of the serious rider and increase his or her ability to position the horse effectively and with finesse. With, of course, the help of the legs, they can counteract deviations and evasions in both quarters and shoulders and they assist materially in reaching the goal exemplified by 'the straight horse'. In fact, the rider who is not familiar with the rein effects is limited in the level of performance he or she will be able to achieve. (There are, of course, those irritating exceptions that prove the rule, the talented 'natural' riders who are able to apply the effects unconsciously and whose heads are refreshingly empty of equestrian theory, but there are *very* few of them.)

The difference between *direct* and *indirect* reins is that the former act on the same side of the horse on which the rein is applied. Indirect reins influence the opposite side to that on which they are applied.

A rein of *opposition* obstructs, blocks or opposes the forward thrust of movement on the side on which it is applied. That movement, if sustained, is then re-channelled by the rein's

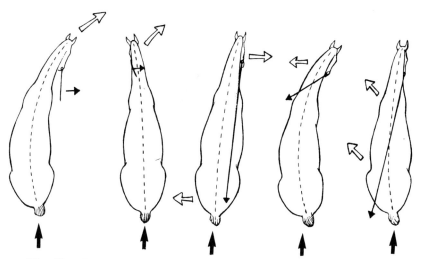

The Five Rein Effects: (*from left to right*) direct or opening rein; indirect rein; direct rein of opposition; indirect rein of opposition in front of the withers; indirect rein of opposition behind the withers

action, either through the shoulders or the quarters, or, in the fifth rein effect, through both.

There are two direct reins and three that are indirect. Three of the five reins act in opposition to re-channel the movement.

The *direct, opening rein* is used on turns and circles when the horse is bent to the inside, the head and neck being aligned to the direction of the movement. It is the easiest turning aid for the young horse to understand and, to a lesser degree, the opening effect is retained in more advanced work.

The *indirect rein* is a neck rein, and it can be used with either one or both hands. Although the primary action is against the neck, there is also a movement of the bit in the mouth. Applied on the left side of the neck the rein moves the right shoulder forward and to the right and vice-versa. It is used in turns and elements of circles asking for an *outside* bend, as would be the case in turn on the forehand, for instance. Obedience to the indirect rein is an essential accomplishment of the polo pony.

The *direct rein of opposition* opposes the movement on the side on which it is applied, i.e. when the right rein is used, the thrust from the quarters, generated by the legs, is blocked on the *right* side of the mouth. In consequence the quarters are shifted to the *left*. This rein effect is used in the forehand turn and (with both hands) in the rein-back.

In fact, while this rein is recommended in instruction, it is very rarely used correctly and more often than not it causes hand and leg to be at cross purposes to the extent that the horse's rhythm is interrupted and the stride of the inside foreleg restricted. The fault may well lie in the strength of the hand, but some of the blame has to lie with the rider's lack of understanding of the consequences arising from the use of an opposing rein.

The instruction most usually given is for the rider to act with the inside rein to effect a turn through the element of a circle represented by the corner of the schooling area. The outside hand is held in support of its acting partner. This is fine, as long as we define *support* correctly. It should mean that the rein, while remaining in contact, should 'be given', so as to allow (support) the inside bend. Too often, 'support' is interpreted as providing a *fixed* base against which the acting hand operates. The movement is then irrevocably restricted.

The instruction insists, rightly enough, on the inside leg acting to provide the necessary impulsion, but it also calls for the outside leg (the *supporting* leg) to act, or at least to be held firmly, behind the girth to prevent the outward swing of the quarters off the track made by the forefeet, although this outward swing has, in fact, *been caused* by the very action of the inside rein! It is simply not logical to create a problem by one action and then seek to correct it by another. In this instance, hand and leg are most certainly at cross purposes.

The right way to ride a circle, or the element of one, is first to increase the impulsion without increasing the speed. As the curve is entered, greater emphasis is given to the *inside leg* while the *inside rein* is *opened* a little with absolutely no pressure being exerted to the rear. The *outside rein* (the supporting rein) is then *lengthened* to allow the bend, by the rider advancing the *outside* hand, elbow, shoulder *and* hip, at which point the body of the rider will conform to the movement of the horse – and Caprilli would not have disagreed with that.

The principle is that of riding from *inside leg* to *outside hand*.

However well performed, this will probably still cause a slight shift of the quarters to the outside and that will need to be held by the outside leg, but we should avoid tying the horse in knots (physically and mentally too, I suspect) by the incorrect and restrictive use of the rein – for rein, read hand and/or, bit. It's all the same thing.

The *indirect rein of opposition in front of the withers* moves the shoulders, the right rein pushing them to the left and vice-versa. However, there is also a secondary movement of the quarters in the opposite direction. Finally, there is the *indirect rein of opposition behind the withers*. This most powerful of reins is also called the intermediate rein or, more grandly, the 'Queen of Reins'. It moves the whole horse sideways and forwards and is used, obviously, for lateral movements.

A word of warning!
The great danger for the novice rider is to think that any one rein can be used in isolation. It cannot. Each rein has to be supported effectively by its partner to moderate or increase the action. In perfection, the rein effects are melded into one harmonious whole. They are effective only when there is ample sustained impulsion and they are *always*, therefore, subordinate to the action of the legs and the impulsion produced by them.

One of the great benefits to be obtained from understanding the rein (or bit) effects is that riders are then in a position to recognise an incorrect use of the rein or one that is in contradiction to the movement required. All too often we see the rein carried over the wither to frustrate the movement being asked of the horse.

Gait and Outline

The bit, in concert with the driving influence of the legs and seat, is used to regulate the gait and effect the transitions, both upwards and downwards.

To regulate the gait, the legs drive the horse into the hand, the fingers closing intermittently on the rein. To make the downward transitions, the same procedure is followed. To move upwards from one gait to the next, i.e. from walk to trot, the

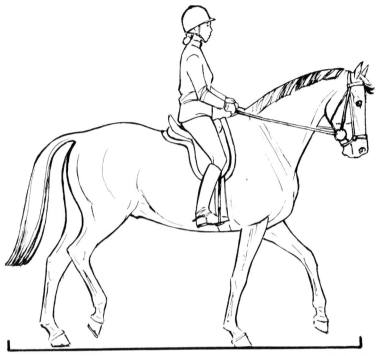

(*Above and opposite page*) The bit preceded by the legs helps in
shortening or lengthening the outline

horse is prepared for the change by the legs pushing upwards to
the bit and then by the fingers easing to allow the horse to move
through from the forward urging of the legs.

In effect, the preparation of the horse for such a request
amounts to a *half-halt*, an action that can be used to reimpose
the balance within any gait. To execute the half-halt, the rider
increases the driving influence of the back, seat and legs and
almost simultaneously raises the hands a little and closes the
fingers. The result is to engage the quarters more actively under
the body, raising and lightening the forehand and effecting a
redistribution of the weight to the rear.

To *shorten* the outline and the horse's base, the legs push

forward into the fingers which resist intermittently and very
tactfully. The horse has then to work within the frame dictated
by the legs at one end and the bit at the other. To *extend*, the
legs continue to act while the fingers give to the degree
necessary.

There is a very recent school of thought which condemns the
half-halt as a movement which will cause the horse to hollow the
back.

One can only presume that the supporters of this argument
have neither learnt how to perform the movement correctly nor
appreciated its application. If the hand were to precede the
action of the legs, or if it was too heavy, or the pressure

prolonged beyond a momentary application of the closing fingers then the horse will probably hollow his back in resistance. But that has nothing to do with a half-halt.

3: The Five Main Groups of Bits

While there are literally thousands of permutations on the basic bitting theme, the principles involve five main groups of bits that exert pressure on one or more of seven parts of the horse's head. If the bit is properly applied by a rider who has learnt to influence the horse through the media of legs, back and seat, the horse moves under control and within the permitted outline.

The five bit groupings are: *snaffle*, *double bridle*, *Pelham*, *gag* and *nose bridle*. The latter is also known as a bitless bridle or, less correctly but more generally, as a hackamore.

Their areas of action are the *corners of the lips*, the *bars*, the *tongue*, the *curb groove*, the *poll*, the *roof of the mouth* and the *nose* in the case of a bitless bridle or when a particular auxiliary piece of equipment is employed. The action may be strengthened or altered by the addition of auxiliaries such as nosebands, martingales, etc.

The pressures applied through the bit to the head vary in intensity and character in accordance with four factors:

1 The construction of the bit;
2 The conformation of the mouth;
3 The angle at which the mouth is carried in relation to the hand;
4 The type and fitting of any accessory to the main bit action that may be used.

The action and pressures concerned, and the results obtained, are, in accordance with the rider's ability to use the supporting aids.

It follows that an understanding of the subject involves a study of:

1 The types of bit available, the varied construction of bits within the group and the resultant action of each;
2 The parts of the head affected and the consequence of pressure being applied to them;
3 The alteration of the bit's action caused by the fitting of auxiliaries, and the types involved;
4 The conformation of the mouth.

The Snaffle

The snaffle is the largest of the five bitting groups. Despite its numerous subdivisions, it is still the least complicated in its action.

There are hundreds of variations on the basic snaffle theme, all of them seeking to improve the quality of the action or to add to it. These differences in the construction of mouthpieces and cheeks can be seen as efforts to make the bit speak louder or more clearly, or perhaps, to speak with no more than an altered accent. Quite a lot of them are successful; others, in particular those that I class as strong bits, may do more harm than good.

Action
Whatever the construction of the snaffle, its primary action is

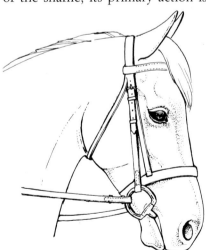

Snaffle bridle with eggbutt
bit and plain cavesson
noseband

upwards against the corners of the lips and in that sense it is believed to encourage the young horse to raise its head. That, of course, is far from being the whole story. The action of the bit is altered very considerably by the addition of auxiliaries, like nosebands and martingales, and, in addition, by the outline assumed by the horse in accordance with its stage of training. Essentially, therefore, the action of the snaffle bit is changed by the position of the head and the relationship of the mouth to the rider's hand.

In the elementary stages of training, when the young horse is long, low and still to an extent on its forehand, the snaffle will certainly slide upwards against the corners of the lips in a lifting action.

As the horse approaches a working outline, however, when the head carriage is higher and the face nearer to the vertical plane, the bit acts more across the lower jaw, encouraging a retraction of the nose, and exerting less pressure on the corners of the lips.

In the advanced horse, carrying its head on, or very close to, the vertical, the action is almost entirely across the lower jaw, even though there will still be a slight upward movement against the corners of the lips.

'Across the lower jaw' involves the bit bearing on the tongue and part of the bars of the mouth. To what extent it bears on either depends on the type of bit used, and the size and shape of the tongue. When a conventional snaffle is employed, the tongue will always overlap the bars by a little, thus protecting them from direct pressure by the bit.

Group divisions

The principal division in the snaffle group is between the unbroken mouthpiece, either a **straight bar** or a **mullen** (half-moon), and the **jointed** mouthpiece made either with a single joint or with a central spatula or a ring link separating the two halves of the mouthpiece. Examples of these are the **French bradoon**, employing a spatula, and the **Dick Christian** (named after a famous Leicestershire foxhunter of the nineteenth century), which uses a ring link.

Of the two, the shaped mullen mouthpiece has to be

The French bradoon with a spatula joint

regarded as the mildest, particularly when it is made of rubber or covered with nylon. Its bearing is largely on the tongue, which lies over, and gives protection to, the bars. A straight bar metal mouthpiece is more usually associated with a stallion bridle rather than with riding, but the conventional 'breaking' or mouthing bit for young horses is often of this type, with loose 'mouthing keys' set in the centre. Mouthing bits can, however, also be jointed, the keys being set on a central ring. Considerable care needs to be taken in the fitting of a mouthing bit if the mouth is not to be damaged or an evasion (like that of putting the tongue over the bit) is not to be encouraged.

Keys will help the horse to keep its mouth wet (i.e. to salivate) by encouraging it to play with them (i.e. to 'mouth' the bit), but many modern trainers prefer to use a nylon or rubber mouthpiece, or the excellent German-type mouthpiece made of soft, moulded plastic, that is discussed later. The argument against the use of the key bit is that the continual mouthing may become habitual and result in an unsteady head carriage.

Youngstock, particularly boisterous young Thoroughbred colts, are often led on a ring bit like the one known as **Tattersall's ring bit**, the lead rein being fastened to the rear of

The Tattersall ring bit

the bit behind the jaws. It is fitted with mouthing keys but is, none the less, a pretty powerful means of restraint.

Chifney's lead bit has an inward curve on the ring's mouthpiece and the lead rein is fastened to the rear. It is lighter and therefore sharper than the Tattersall ring. Its full name is Chifney's anti-rear lead bit. I can think of nothing *less* likely to discourage that sort of behaviour, nor anything *more* likely to provoke a horse into rearing against the discomfort.

Samuel Chifney (1753–1807) was a competent, if enormously conceited, jockey. Among his successes was the 1789 Derby, which he won on Skyscraper. Writing about himself in 1773, he averred, 'I can ride horses in a better manner in a race to beat others than any person ever known in my time.' Two years later, he wrote, 'I can train horses for running better than any person I knew in my time.' He wrote in much the same vein about the range of bits that bore his name, many of which were as ridiculous as his anti-rear bit. In later life, Chifney was involved in a number of scandals and he died in virtual penury, his name surviving only in the Derby records and through his anti-rear bit.

A jointed mouthpiece is necessarily more direct in its action because of the 'nutcracker' effect over the lower jaw. The joint allows room for the tongue, rather in the same fashion as the port in the mouth of a curb bit, and so the mouthpiece is able to bear on the outward sides of the bars but not directly on the sensitive top edges. When a spatula or link is employed, the nutcracker action is reduced commensurately. The bit lies comfortably over the tongue and there is possibly less direct pressure on the outside of the bars.

A recently introduced range of excellently made German snaffles provides a more direct emphasis. The mouthpiece is ported, somewhat like that of a curb bit, but broader and not so deep. It therefore allows room for the tongue and must, on that account alone, put a more direct pressure on the top of the bars. As long as the horse is carrying its head in approximately a working position, contact on the corners of the lips is avoided. (These bits are logical in their design and very good for horses at a medium level of training. However, on reading a description of the bits in an English catalogue, I am not certain that their action is properly appreciated.)

Diameter
The diameter of the mouthpiece is critical to the action. Broad, thick mouthpieces are more effective than narrow, pencil-thin varieties. A broad mouthpiece bears upon a correspondingly large number of sensory nerves, the nerves of feeling that are very close to the surface in the mouth, lips and tongue. The sensory nerves end in the brain at the centres of memory and consciousness. Because it is so sharp, the narrow mouthpiece obtains a swift initial response, but very soon the concentrated pressure over so small an area results in the nerves becoming numb or deadened and that part of the mouth becomes insensitive and can sometimes even become calloused. The horse may then be condemned as hard-mouthed and a puller. All too often, more ironmongery is put in the mouth, a stronger bit is employed, and matters go from bad to worse. The answer is to fit the softest and thickest bit that can be found, on the principle that horses pull against pain and become more responsive when fitted with a comfortable bitting arrangement like that given by the German plastic mouthpieces. It is also as well to remind oneself of the adage that it takes two to pull. Otherwise, if all else fails, you may commend your soul to your Maker while pretending that you really do want to go that fast!

The cheeks
Snaffles can be made with a number of cheeks or bit-rings. The most common is the **loose ring**, which passes through a hole in the end of the mouthpiece. It allows movement of the bit in the mouth, encouraging salivation and, as long as the ring is large enough, it will assist the lateral movement of the head by pressing up against the cheek in response to tension from the rein on the opposite side. If the bit is fitted correctly, a large ring goes some way towards countering any tendency for the horse to evade the central action by sliding the bit through its mouth.

The disadvantage of the loose ring is that it can pinch the lips between the ring and the hole through which it passes. Should the hole become enlarged or roughened with wear, the possibility of pinching is very much increased.

To avoid pinching of this sort the deservedly popular **eggbutt** snaffle is used. This will not pinch nor can it slide through the mouth easily, but the amount of possible movement is much reduced. The inability of the horse to play with the mouthpiece may be an advantage or it could prove an undesirable feature if the horse is inclined to be dry in its mouth, causing stiffness in the lower jaw and preventing its relaxation.

Logically, the most effective eggbutt is one with a slot cut in the ring to accommodate the bridle cheek. This ensures that the bit is fixed centrally in the mouth and that its action is directed more across the lower jaw than the corners of the lips. Alas, this pattern seems to have gone out of fashion and production.

The eggbutt derived from the **dee-cheek** racing snaffle, which, in turn, was modified from the **full cheek** snaffle. The cheeks prevent the bit from sliding through the mouth and, of course, also assist in persuading the horse to turn its head one way or the other, by pressing up against the animal's face. Racing men discarded them in favour of the dee-cheek because, *in extremis*, it was just possible for the end of a cheek to be pushed up a nostril.

Unlike its fixed-cheek predecessor, the modern cheek snaffle, the Australian loose-ring pattern popularly known as the **Fulmer snaffle**, allows some movement in the mouthpiece, although this is largely prevented by the retaining straps fitted from the bridle cheek to the upperpart of the bit cheek in order to maintain the bit's position in the mouth. These retainers

Fulmer or Australian loose ring, cheek snaffle

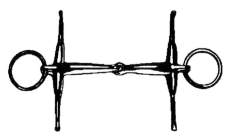

would, of course, also prevent the end of the cheek entering the nostril.

Materials

Most of today's bits are made from stainless steel, which is reliable and easily cleaned.

(In the nineteenth century, and even between the wars, bits were made from forged steel and corrosion was a major problem. Bits had to be cleaned and polished very frequently. If they became rusted, they had to be burnished with a chain mail pad and a mixture of sand and oil. Curb chains were kept in good order by being 'swung' in a stable rubber with a little dampened sand.)

Mouthpieces may be made softer by being covered in rubber, nylon, etc., and one German firm makes a range of bits using a flexible plastic mouthpiece that conforms softly and continuously to the shape of the lower jaw, at whatever angle the jaw may be held. The mouthpiece is tapered at its centre, removing any uncomfortable bearing on the tongue and doing away with the need for that potentially damaging central joint in the conventional snaffle. Forty-odd years ago, sensitive, highly strung horses were being ridden in a mouthpiece made, on much the same principle, from thick, softened rawhide. (I have never met a horse that is allergic to metal but if there is one I am assured that the German mouthpiece will do the trick.)

Another mouthpiece incorporates copper, usually in the form of rollers fitted round the mouthpiece. The rollers help, one supposes, to keep the mouth moist, while the copper, it is claimed, is 'warmer' in the mouth. To what degree that can be substantiated is arguable, but the old *vaqueros* of South America used copper, as well as a little gold, for essentially the same purpose and horsemen of past times used to warm the mouthpiece of the bit in their hands before putting it in the mouth of a young horse. (I used to wrap a treacle-soaked bandage round the mouthpiece – but it's very messy!)

The 'stoppers'

Quite the opposite to the plastic mouthpiece, both in principle and practice, are those bits that can be called strong. Many of them, though now more streamlined in form, closely resemble those overtly powerful bits of ancient civilisations.

An obvious way in which to increase the severity of a bit is to **twist** the mouthpiece. That is bad enough, but when the mouthpiece is of twisted 'wire' it becomes less acceptable.

Following the practice of horsemen long ago, the bit can be made more powerful by the addition of **rollers** round the mouthpiece. The idea is to prevent the horse from taking a firm hold of the bit (the 'bit between its teeth') and to encourage it to relax its lower jaw by mouthing the rollers. It is probably less severe than it appears at first sight. Nor am I convinced that rollers inset across the mouthpiece, after the fashion of the **Magenis** bit, deserve their reputation as a harsh deterrent to the wayward horse – not, that is, if the hands at the other end are educated ones, but then even a broad, soft snaffle becomes an instrument of torture in heavy hands.

The Magenis mouthpiece is often squared off at its edges, a practice that could cause a problem, but if it is rounded instead, this bit is by no means fierce in experienced hands and works very well with the horse that has learnt to evade by crossing its jaws. The late Lieutenant-Colonel Jack Talbot-Ponsonby (winner of the King George V Gold Cup at London's Royal International Show on three occasions: 1930, 1932 and 1934) used the Magenis quite frequently. Indeed, for a while it became known as Talbot-Ponsonby's bit. He explained that it should be used in a soft, gliding motion across the mouth, the action being caused by using the fingers of each hand alternately *and*, of course, in conjunction with the legs.

The result was to make the horse drop its nose and relax the lower jaw. Although the bit appears in Benjamin Latchford's *The Loriner* under the name Magenis, it is possible that this is a

The Magenis roller snaffle

corruption of the name MacGuiness, another of those hard-riding Meltonians.

The **Scorrier**, or **Cornish snaffle**, has no such pretensions to gentility. It is simply a strong, restraining force calculated to stop even the most inveterate of pullers. (I am reminded of the saying, 'You can always stop a horse – the problem is to get him to go again.') The Scorrier is distinguished by having four rings instead of two, an arrangement known as Wilson rings and much used in driving bridles.

The two inside rings are fitted in slots set within the mouthpiece itself, the inside surface of the latter being serrated or grooved for greater effect. The inside rings are attached to the cheekpieces of the bridle, the rein being fastened to the outer rings. This gives greater, direct effect to the rein. When both cheeks and rein fasten to the same ring, in the normal way, the rein pressure is mitigated to some degree by the slight upward restraint of the bridle cheek. In the Scorrier, pressure on the rein produces an inward, squeezing action on the sides of the mouth through the inside rings. That, combined with the powerful rein action and the serrated mouthpiece, amounts to a pretty forceful means of persuasion.

The **Y-mouth** or **W-mouth** snaffle has two mouthpieces, the joints being set one on either side. It is not a pleasant device, nor a sensible one, and is more than likely to cause pinching of the lips and tongue.

I am no more enthusiastic about **spring mouths**, or **butterfly clips**, which are attached to the bit to give a strong, additional action to the mouthpiece.

A simple means of reinforcing the strength of a bridle in times past was a **nose-net**, an item not unlike the net fitted to a calf's nose to prevent it from suckling. Fastened to the cavesson by

Scorrier, or Cornish, snaffle

small straps and adjusted tight up against the muzzle, it had a most remarkable effect on pulling horses. Quite simply, they backed off from it, being unwilling to push their noses into the thing. In consequence, they accepted the bit and stopped pulling! They were used on cab horses by the old cab masters who bought up Thoroughbreds that, for one reason or another, were unsuitable to race. These reprobates were swiftly enough brought to heel by the simple expedient of doubling their working hours and, lest they reverted to their old ways and attempted to take off, by the fitting of the harmless nose-net.

Forgotten but useful
There are two other snaffles worthy of note other than for their curiosity value: indeed, one of them is still generally available. This is the **Fillis** snaffle, used by and named after James Fillis (1834–1913) the apostle of '*la grande impulsion*' and author of *Breaking and Riding* (J. A. Allen). (In fact, Fillis was no scholar and his book was 'ghosted' for him by his pupil, the famous French politician Clemenceau.) Born in London, Fillis went to France at an early age. Along with Baucher, Raabe and a handful of others, he deserves to be numbered among the latter-day masters. He probably schooled more horses to a higher level (36 in the *Haute Ecole*) than any man of his time and he had the distinction of being appointed Colonel and *Ecuyer-en-chef* at the Russian Cavalry School for ten years.

The Fillis snaffle differs from the general run by being suspended in the mouth, as opposed to resting on it. It is jointed at each side of the port, so reducing the squeezing action. The port allows ample room for the largest of tongues. (A factor frequently overlooked in bitting is, indeed, the size of the tongue. Some horses have tongues almost too big for their

Fillis Snaffle

mouths. This is certainly true of some Arabs, in particular those with really tiny muzzles. When this occurs, it causes an obvious problem.) The Fillis, like the German snaffles mentioned earlier, allows room for the tongue and, combined with the suspended nature of the mouthpiece, is considered to be helpful with horses who come 'over' or 'behind' the bit. At one time bits of this suspended type were quite numerous and their action well understood.

Like so many bits, the Fillis snaffle suffers from incorrect nomenclature, usually the fault of catalogue compilers. At least one prominent English firm calls it 'Filet Baucher', a title befitting a steak named in honour of François Baucher perhaps, but having nothing to do with the Fillis snaffle.

Less well-known is the now extinct **Distas** or **Weedon** snaffle. (It was marketed by the firm of Distas and used at the Weedon cavalry school.)

The bit was made with a broad, flat, curved mouthpiece fitted with eggbutt rings made with carefully positioned slots to take the bridle cheeks. The slots ensured that the mouthpiece lay flat over the tongue and across the bars. Its width distributed the pressure over a broad area and it was held to permit a degree of flexion unobtainable in ordinary snaffles. However, the drop noseband, now used so extensively, was not much in evidence then.

Another Weedon device was a training bridle for young horses that employed a four-ring snaffle, a noseband being attached between the inside rings. For some reason it was called a **Newmarket bridle**, even at Weedon, but I never saw anything like it in use at the headquarters of racing. The bridle was used to obtain a lowered position of the nose, using either one or two reins, before introducing work in a double bridle, and this is what Brigadier Bowden-Smith, a pre-war Olympic rider and an instructor at Weedon, had to say about it:

> It is an excellent form of snaffle for training a young horse for it can be adjusted to take a considerable amount of pressure on the nose, thus saving the sensitive young mouth. By using the rein on the top or noseband ring only, the mouth can be completely rested.

The bridle is vastly superior to any combination of cavesson and snaffle*, with one pair of reins attached to the rings of the cavesson and one pair to the snaffle. This is a cumbersome contrivance and makes horses' noses and lips sore!

Pre-war horsemen do not seem to have been so concerned with closing the mouth in order to prevent evasion of the bit, and the Newmarket bridle had no provision for doing so. Perhaps that is why it seems to have worked so well as a schooling bridle.

The remaining bridles belong to the racing world and are essentially sophisticated versions of the Weedon bridle, although they employ a central face strap, fastened to the nosepiece, that is capable of being adjusted to raise the bit in the mouth.

The **Rockwell** is the milder of the two. It has a thickish snaffle on the mouthpiece to which is fitted a metal figure-of-eight link. The top loops have an adjustable elastic nosepiece attached to them. This, in turn, is supported by a strap running up by the nose, through a central slot on the browband and fastening to the bridle head. The head is lowered by a combination of nose and bit pressure to give greater control over a hard pulling horse and, additionally, there is the powerful psychological restraint imposed by the divided central strap running up the face.

The **Norton** (also called the Citation after a famous race-horse) is more severe and is closer to the Scorrier in its action. However, unlike the latter, it employs two mouthpieces, the secondary one being of the thin wire sort. The noseband is attached to this sharp mouthpiece by means of metal loops

---

*A reference to the practice dating from the Renaissance schools, which was, at that time, still practised at the German cavalry schools and at the Spanish School in Vienna.

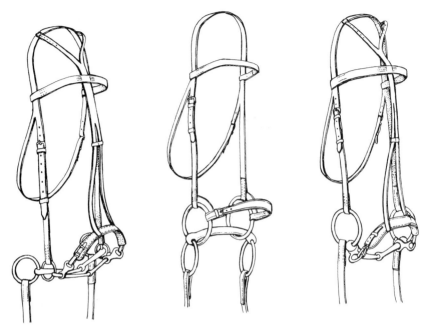

Bridles: (*left to right*) Norton, Newmarket and Rockwell

connected to the inner rings – all in all, a powerful piece of equipment.

The Ultimate Bridle

If the snaffle is the most simple form of control, the **double bridle** is the most complex in its action and the most productive in terms of suggesting the carriage of the head. It is the bridle for the educated horse and with it the educated rider can convey the finer nuances of communication with a finesse not possible through any other bitting system.

It comprises a bradoon (a light, jointed snaffle having either small rings or a small eggbutt cheek) and a curb bit to which a curb chain can be attached. In the past there were a great many patterns of curb bit: Weymouth, Ward Union, Leicester,

Melton, Dick Christian, Thurlow, Chifney, Harry Highover and all. Today, despite the best efforts of the catalogue compilers to confuse us by assigning names incorrectly or misspelling them, we differentiate between fixed-cheek and slide- or turn-cheek curbs; between thick (or **German**) mouthpieces and the lighter **'Cambridge'** mouths, which may vary in their diameter; and we call a short cheek, i.e. one not over 90 mm (3½ in) in length, a **Tom Thumb**.

Less distinction is made between the variations that can and still do occur in the shape of the port and in the length of cheek in relation to the width of the mouthpiece and to its length *above* and *below* the mouthpiece. This is a pity, as these are factors that ought to be considered when selecting a bit.

Action
When operated by practised fingers, the bradoon can be used to raise the head should it be necessary to correct the carriage.

The curb and its attendant chain have a much wider application. When, in response to the rein, the curb bit assumes an angle of 45 degrees in the mouth, that part of the cheek above the mouthpiece, which incorporates the eye, moves forward on its permitted arc. It therefore exerts a downward pressure on the *poll* through the cheekpiece to which it is attached. (The quoted cheek angle of 45 degrees is generally accepted. Clearly, however, the angle at which the bit is brought into play depends on the tightness or otherwise of the curb chain. If the curb chain is adjusted fairly tightly, the bit will

Curb bit (fixed cheek) and bradoon fitted with lipstrap

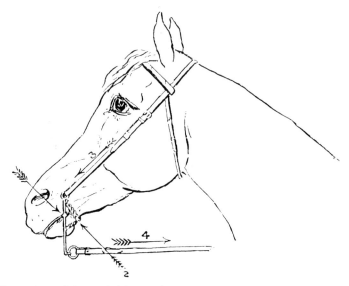

The action of the curb bit as a lever

come into action earlier, possibly when the angle of the cheek approaches about 30 degrees. If no further pressure is applied to the rein in order to increase that angle [which is as it should be], the amount of poll pressure exerted would be commensurately less.)

Simultaneously, the curb chain tightens in the curb groove to encourage a relaxation (flexion) of the lower jaw, a retraction of the nose and a corresponding flexion at the poll.

The mouthpiece then puts pressure on the tongue and the bars, the distribution of the pressure varying according to the shape of the tongue and the dimensions of the port, the raised curve in the centre of the mouthpiece. The effect is down and to the rear.

It is obvious that the manner in which pressure is exerted and the intensity of that pressure depends on the construction of the bit, and that, both in theory and practice, should depend upon the conformation of the mouth.

In simple terms, the severity of the bit depends on:
1 The length of the cheek;
2 The adjustment of the curb chain;
3 The shape of the ported mouthpiece;

Poll pressure increases or decreases according to the length of the cheek above the mouthpiece. To conform with the principle of levers, but, more important, to ensure that the mouthpiece lies and acts in the mouth without causing discomfort, it is taken that the length of the cheek above the mouthpiece should be 44 mm (1¾ in). The cheek below the mouthpiece should be twice as long as the upper one, i.e. 88 mm (3½ in), giving an overall height of 132 mm (5¼ in). In fact, the total length of the cheek in most production bits will follow the rule of thumb that calls for the length of the cheek to equal the width of the mouthpiece. Usually, it is not too far wrong but it is, on the other hand, a result obtained more by luck than informed judgement.

There are horses who do not take kindly to poll pressure, in which case the length of the cheek would need to be less. Whether it should ever be longer than the recommended 44 mm (1¾ in) is problematical. Horsemen of previous generations, almost to a man, condemned the use of poll pressure as being contrary to the pure principles of working from the relaxation of the lower jaw. They considered it to be a coercive force that made the goal of lightness in the hand impossible to achieve. (The more I think about it and the older I get, the more I find myself in agreement.)

A cheek extending to more than 88 mm (3½ in) below the mouthpiece increases the possible leverage and risks damaging the mouth. A shorter cheek, like the Tom Thumb, reduces leverage and would be more appropriate in a hypersensitive mouth.

The tighter the curb chain, the less tension will be required on the rein to produce pressure on the bars, tongue and curb groove. This is where the length of the upper cheek becomes critical. It must be just long enough to draw the curb chain exactly into the groove when the rein is applied. If it is too long it pulls the curb chain upwards out of the groove and onto the unprotected jaw bones. Constant irritation here causes the horse to resist by poking its nose. Conversely, a curb chain adjusted too loosely will be just as bad as it, too, will rise out of the curb groove. The proper length of the curb chain, excluding the curb hooks, has been calculated as being about 25 per cent longer than the width of the mouthpiece.

The shape of the port governs the pressure exerted on the tongue and bars. A very shallow port, or a mullen mouthpiece, places more emphasis on the tongue and less on the bars. A deeper port, allowing more room for the tongue and preventing it from overlapping the bars, allows for an increase of pressure on the bars and a more direct bearing on their top part. A very high port may come into contact with the roof of the mouth, the results of which can be imagined! Such bits are used in some parts of the world but they have no place in the system of European riding.

The golden rule, now long forgotten, was that the width of the port should be equal to the tongue channel or groove, i.e. the space under the tongue between the inside of the bars. If it was narrower it would not admit the tongue, and if wider it would reduce the bearing surface of the mouthpiece, which was intended to act on the bars. More than one authority gave the desirable width (suitable for almost every horse) as being 33 mm (1⅓ in), this measure being based on the fact that the tongue channel is generally three-quarters of the height of the bars and that the latter could be taken as being 45 mm (1⅘ in).

Whether the cheek is fixed or loose (with the ability to slide up and down) is also significant. It might be thought that the loose cheek is less severe, allowing as it does for movement in the mouth. In fact, the contrary is true as it allows something like an extra 12 mm (½ in) of leverage when the curb is brought into use. Furthermore, the action is very likely to be uneven and imprecise unless both cheeks slide up and down with equal ease, and that does not always happen.

It will be seen that the fitting of the curb bit is a matter to be approached with care if numerous pitfalls are to be avoided and the horse's mouth is to remain undamaged. Thereafter, the rider needs to learn how to handle the reins in much the same way that a pianist increases his or her dexterity, through finger exercises. Finally, it would seem reasonable to accustom the horse to the varied and very different pressures involved in the double bridle and to do so from the ground before it is ridden in one.

In Britain, many riders hold the bradoon rein outside the little finger. When that is the case, the bradoon tends to predominate. If the curb rein is held in that way, which is more logical as it corresponds to the position of the bits in the mouth, then the curb influence is predominant. Using the reins in this way, the hands are turned a little upwards in a lifting action on the bradoon, and downwards to obtain depression.

Another way to hold the reins is with the bradoon outside the little finger but with the end of the curb rein leaving the hand through the first and second fingers and being held in place by the thumb. The thumb will prevent the bradoon rein slipping through the hand, while the two middle fingers act easily to increase or release pressure on the curb rein. Both methods require practise.

The Banbury

The Banbury is an exception to the conventional patterns of modern curb bits and it often works when the usual patterns fail.

The mouthpiece is a round bar, tapered towards its centre to make it comfortable for the tongue, and fitted with slots cut into

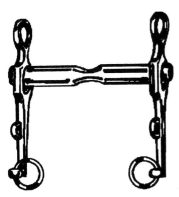

The Banbury Curb with independent cheeks

the cheek. The mouthpiece can thus revolve in the mouth and can also move up and down. This arrangement allows the animal to mouth the bit, so keeping its mouth wet, and it further prevents the horse from taking hold of it. As the cheeks are loose, it is possible to operate each one independently of the other, which is an advantage in certain circumstances, particularly, perhaps, with a horse that resists by stiffening one side of its mouth.

The shape of the mouthpiece and the way in which it can be moved in the mouth does not cause direct pressure on the bars. This very imprecision in the action may be one reason why this curb seems to work well with difficult subjects.

The single curb

It was once fashionable to show hacks in a single-rein curb bridle, without the usual accompaniment of a bradoon. The curb used had an elegant curved cheek and it represented a nice piece of oneupmanship when employed in a class of quality hacks, indicating a high level of training. It is not so much seen today, if at all, but the little Globe cheek curb (sometimes called a Hunloke) still appears in pony show classes.

What very few of us can appreciate today, is that our forefathers (particularly those concerned with the huge cavalry establishment maintained in Europe) were concerned to train horses to be ridden on a curb bit, the addition of a bradoon being looked upon as 'a second string to the bow'.

Dwyer (*Seats and Saddles, Bits and Bitting*) described the bradoon as 'an aid in the early stages of training to facilitate the transition from the snaffle to the curbed bit; and in proportion as the young horse becomes familiar with the latter it is gradually laid aside.'

Cavalry rode on the curb, the bradoon rein looping and exerting no action at all. 'Classical' horsemanship, the basis for the cavalry schools' teaching, was similarly concerned. The bradoon, in fact, at least in Europe, took the place of the Renaissance cavesson. It is interesting to see pictures of Guérinière and engravings by Johann Ridinger that show very clearly exactly such a relationship between curb and bradoon. According to illustrations of the period, that relationship appears to have persisted right up to the end of the nineteenth century at the Spanish Riding School in Vienna.

What is very certain is that horsemen of that era and for some time after, in some instances up to the outbreak of the Second World War, made detailed studies of the science of bitting that were directed at preserving the lightness of the mouth and avoiding any sort of damage or discomfort. Although we have advanced in all sorts of other ways, our knowledge of bitting is minimal in comparison with theirs – and, my goodness, doesn't it show.

Chains and hooks
I believe that curb chains and the hooks by which they are connected to the eye of the bit are of more importance to the successful bitting of the horse than is generally realised. Indeed, it is true to say that 50 per cent of the bit's effectiveness depends upon the proper choice and fitting of the curb chain.

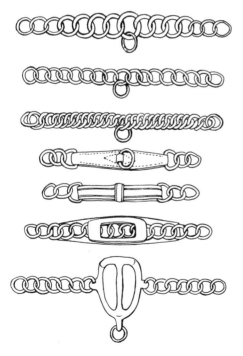

A selection of curb chains: (*top to bottom*) Flat link; Single link; Double link; Leather; Elastic; Curb in rubber curb guard; 'Jodphur' curb

Curb chains are made from linked metal rings, the links being either single or double (so as to provide a continuous smooth mesh), or they can be made of broader, flat links.

In fitting a curb chain, the object is to ensure that it gives the maximum possible comfort to the horse. In this respect, the heavier double chain and the flat-link sort are superior to the single link variety. The chain can be made even softer in its action by using a rubber curb guard, which will also act as a safeguard against chafing.

A curb can also be made from leather, neatly and expensively stitched and with three links on each end. What is probably more satisfactory, and certainly cheaper, is a shaped strip of soft, red buffalo hide made with slits at each end to fasten over the hooks and so dispensing with the metal links. That, along with the doubled elastic pattern, is my personal preference. Both can be fitted very snugly without the risk of causing discomfort and the resilience of the elastic is a further bonus.

All of these types of curb should be fitted with a 'fly' link through which the lip strap can pass. The lip strap helps to prevent the curb chain from rising out of the groove and no double bridle is complete without one.

A frequent source of discomfort and chafing is the curb hook. These are often of lower quality than the bit itself, and poorly

The flat circle curb hook which is comfortable and far less likely to chafe.

made. Those on the German-made bits are better than the general run, being well finished, but even they do not approach the shaped, circle pattern curb hook that lies absolutely flat and will rarely be found to chafe the sensitive skin around the corners of the lips.

The Pelham

The Pelham is no more than a curb bit with a loop at the top end to which an extra rein can be attached. It is the half-way house, if you like, between the snaffle and the double bridle – a compromise that presumes to produce the sophisticated action of the latter by means of two reins acting on a single mouthpiece. However, in both theory and practice this is an impossibility. Furthermore, as the bit is neither wholly curb nor wholly snaffle, there is a problem as to where it should be positioned in the mouth, i.e. high enough just to wrinkle the lips or low enough to act over the bars. The most that can be said in the majority of instances is that when the emphasis is given to the bradoon rein, the action approaches that of a snaffle and when the curb rein is used more strongly, it is the curb that predominates.

In the years between the wars, great ingenuity was expended on the Pelham, the market being swamped with the theories of enthusiasts now translated into metal shapes. It remains a seemingly effective bit for polo ponies but it is otherwise undesirable and is not permissible under FEI and BHS dressage rules.

While the Pelham has disadvantages, however, it also has its good points and it should not be discarded out of hand. Depending on the pattern selected, it can be a useful bit in regaining the confidence of a horse that has suffered a mouth injury and has become frightened as a result. (In my opinion far more horses than we can ever imagine have damaged mouths and thus experience discomfort that, naturally enough, is revealed in their behaviour under saddle.)

Second, it is better suited than a double bridle to cobby-type animals that have short, thick jaw formations, and it is sometimes a better bit to use on Arab horses, too. This type of animal just cannot accommodate two mouthpieces comfortably and the Pelham suits it very well. (Conversely, of course, the Pelham is not as suitable for long-jawed Thoroughbred sorts. In their case, if the bit is placed high enough to be of any use, the curb chain will lie above and out of the curb groove.)

Third, largely because the action of most of the available patterns is soft and imprecise, and thus not too demanding, a number of horses will go very acceptably in them.

For all three reasons, the Pelham is less potentially damaging in the hands of less accomplished riders.

Of the Pelhams available, the usual **mullen mouth**, whether of metal or vulcanite, has no particular merit and has a tendency to chafe the lips and the corners of the mouth.

The **Scamperdale** overcomes this problem by having the mouthpiece turned back at each end to bring the cheeks an inch or so back and away from the usual area of chafing. The action, of course, is mainly on the tongue. Some pressure can be put over the bars by using a **Hartwell mouth**, which is no more than an arch mouth or the usual ported mouth found in a curb bit.

The **S.M.** (Sam Marsh) Pelham, also appears as the **Faudel Phillips** Pelham. Both these horsemen/teachers used this bit but it did, in fact, originate in the United States and was imported to Britain by the Distas Saddlery Company in the 1930s. It has a broad, flat mouthpiece with a port, and its cheeks move independently in a restricted arc (restricted because of a small stud set on the mouthpiece, which also has the same degree of movement). This Pelham has its faults but was not unsuccessful in its day.

As good as any pattern is the **Rugby**, which has an independent link for the bradoon rein. It allows stronger and more clearly defined poll and curb pressure and has the characteristics of a curb bit rather than otherwise.

The difficulty with Pelhams is that the top bradoon ring compels the cheek above the mouth to be made longer – usually too long. Furthermore, the top ring can interfere with the action of the curb chain and in most instances it is probably better to put the curb chain through the bradoon ring to keep it in place. (The link on the Rugby is the solution to those problems.)

Pelhams can be made, and were, with every sort of

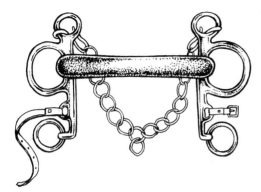

Vulcanite Mullen
mouth Pelham
fitted with lipstrap

Port Mouth Hartwell
Pelham

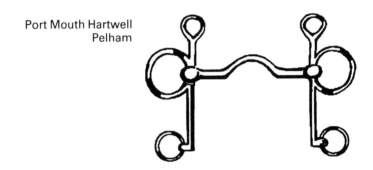

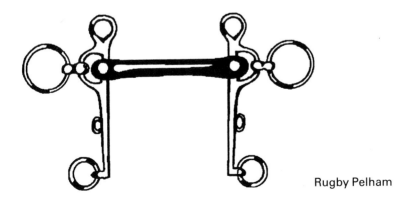

Rugby Pelham

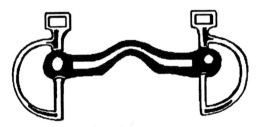

The single rein Kimblewick, first known in England as the Spanish Jumping bit

mouthpiece and in one or two strange shapes, but one notable member of the group cannot be overlooked. It is the **Kimblewick**, which started life as an adaptation of a Spanish pattern bit used for jumping. The first Englishman to promote its use was the late Phil Oliver, father of Alan, and it was called Kimblewick after the Buckinghamshire village in which he lived.

Its action differs from that of most Pelhams because the eye is squared off. As a result, the downward poll pressure is increased substantially. When the hand is lowered, the rein slips down the ring and the rein tension produces immediate and direct poll pressure combined with a fairly strong downward action on the bars. As a result, the head is dropped and the mouth comes below the level of the hand.

This bit can most certainly cause bruising in heavy hands and for that reason I would rather that it was not used by children (whose hands can sometimes be more enthusiastic than sensitive). If overemployed, I think it causes a horse to hang on the bit, but it can be useful as a 'change' bit for exuberant subjects on special occasions.

I have never seen any good purpose served by a **jointed mouth** Pelham, which if it is to be effective, needs to have an unacceptably tight curb chain, nor do I think it is very sensible to join the two rings with a leather rounding so as to ride on a single rein. It is a little more intelligent to have a rein that divides into two 30 cm (12 in) or so from the bit, the lower strap being adjustable so as to deliver a constant curb pressure – but only a little.

The most effective type of divided rein to use with a Pelham

Pelham roundings allow the rider to use a single rein but are not otherwise a very sensible arrangement

The Gag

Very early in the people/horse relationship, riders appreciated that control was better obtained when the horse's mouth was held a little lower than the hand and for centuries much thought was given to bits and auxiliaries that lowered the head and brought the nose inwards.

The gag bits depart from that accepted practice by doing just the opposite – they are used to lift the head. It could be argued that the construction, a rounded leather or cord cheekpiece

Gag bridle with a top rein fitted to the ring

passing through holes in the bit rings, produces effects in opposition to each other. If the bit is raised upwards in the mouth it is only logical to suppose that an equal downward pressure is put on the poll via the bridle head – a classic instance of both ends acting against the middle, the middle in this case being that part of the head between the corners of the lips and the poll. For practical purposes, it can be taken that a gag bridle accentuates the upward action of the snaffle to act as a head-raiser. Clearly, of course, there is also a further, restraining pressure to the rear.

It has a place in modern equitation, most particularly in cross-country events when lightweight riders on big, fit, high-couraged horses can draw some comfort from its presence. Perhaps, also, it is the bridle for the 'fallen angel' that approaches its fences very fast with its head either tucked into its chest or held firmly between its knees. If its use goes some way to avoiding accident and injury, the gag bridle is legitimate enough in those circumstances. However, it is always advisable to put an additional rein on the bit ring itself, riding on that and using the gag only occasionally and when necessary. Otherwise, there is a likelihood of the bit becoming less effective as the horse becomes familiar with it.

The Nose Bridle

Last of the bridle groups is that which dispenses with the bit, relying for its effect on pressure on the nose. For this reason it is known as a **bitless** bridle or, more usually, as a **hackamore**, a misnomer now firmly established within the bosom of equestrian vocabulary.

This bridle derives from the nose-to-bit system of the Iberian horsemen, in which the horse was trained and, if you like, mouthed initially from its nose; control passing gradually from the noseband to a potentially severe bit. This is the basis of the true hackamore system, of which a short explanation is given in the following pages.

A simple form of bitless bridle can be made from a drop-noseband fitted with a couple of rings for the reins. It is not much more difficult to make up a basic nose bridle and use it as

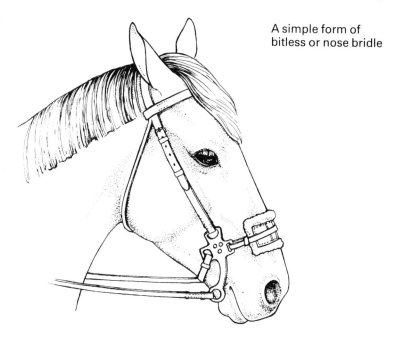

A simple form of
bitless or nose bridle

a training bridle on the Iberian principle, gradually transferring control to the bit.

Bitless bridles can also be used to advantage as 'rest' bridles for horses that have suffered damage to their mouths. However, most bitless bridles are used by long-distance riders and some, of course, by showjumpers. The Americans, naturally enough, produce some excellent patterns.

Control is obtained primarily through direct pressure on the nose but in some patterns there is also curb action and possibly some poll pressure too. The strength of the bridle depends upon the length of the cheeks. Most are operated on a single rein but at least one, the **William Stone** pattern, is designed for use with two reins and is, in fact, termed a bitless Pelham, the lower rein operating the curb. (William Stone worked as a bit-maker in Walsall with the firm of Matthew Harvey. He had a deep knowledge of bit patterns as well as an enquiring and inventive mind. He was responsible for the renewed manufacture of a number of bits that had gone out of production, as well as producing a number of items on his own account.)

The Hackamore explained

Those items of headgear comprising *la jaquima* (the hacka-more), along with the high speed pivots, sliding stops, squaw-reining and roll-backs of the Western horseman, have no relevance in European ('Eastern', 'English seat') riding, unless it is in the training of the polo pony, and then only in part.

None the less the tack (i.e. the 'tackle' associated with training and riding) and the system of schooling to which the hackamore is integral, derive from sophisticated training methods of balance and control that belong to a far older, possibly more skilful and certainly no less legitimate school of riding than that to which we have become accustomed.

It was, in essence, the basis and inspiration of the classical schools, in which, for all their faults, the final goal was lightness in hand. (Today, the Holy Grail of riding, that quality of supreme lightness in hand, has almost been eclipsed by competitive considerations. To a degree it remains in the French school, where once it dominated equestrian thinking: it still survives, possibly in its purest form, in Spain and Portugal, and also in the Soviet Union, where the pervasive influence of James Fillis is still evident.)

Long before the invention of the curb bit by the Celts of Gaul in about 400 BC, and its subsequent extension into the seemingly horrendously long-cheeked bits of the Middle Ages, a robust riding tradition existed in countries of the Middle and Far East, which emphasised control and submission through pressure on the nose and head rather than on the mouth. It still persists today in the Middle East, where horses are ridden by means of a single thick rope of woven wool attached to light chains encircling the nose. A painting by Henry Bernard Chalon, of 'George IV's Persian Horses Being Taken out for Exercise' (they are, in fact, indubitably Arabian), that can be seen in the Sporting Art section of London's Tate Gallery, clearly shows a more sophisticated version of the same theme, in which the action of the bit is assisted by the use of such nose

The Western 'Hackamore': *bosal* (noseband), *latigo* (headstall), *fiador* (throat latch), *mecate* (reins) and the heel knot

Method of attaching the *mecate* to the heel knot of the *bosal* in a series of 'wraps'

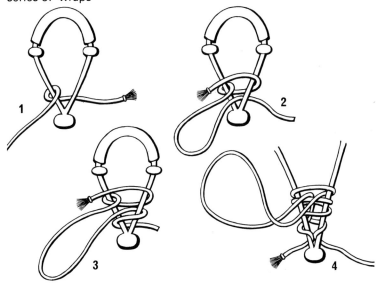

chains. The arrangement is reminiscent of that used on the American cow-pony, except that on the cow-pony the bit is often supported by a light rawhide noseband or *bosal* rather than a chain. (Today in Italy, horses drawing the *fiacres* are driven solely from the nose by means of a cavesson that is fitted on each side with a ring, set on a short projecting metal shank, to which the reins are attached.)

That there should be so close a similarity between the New World and the Eastern element of the Old is not surprising. During the Moorish occupation of the Iberian Peninsula in the seventh and eighth centuries, a system of horse schooling evolved that was based on *la jaquima*, from which the word 'hackamore' is derived. It was directed at the production of a practical dressage horse that performed at speed, in response to the weight of a looping rein attached to a high-ported curb bit and the precise distribution of the rider's weight, and was used either in combat or when working the fierce, long-horned black cattle that are still traditional to the area. The horses are ridden in one hand and the system continues to perpetuate the difference between the forward-riding Eastern horsemen and his European counterpart who sat and thought backwards.

Eight hundred years after the defeat of the Moors by Charles Martel and his knights at Poitiers in AD 720, the Spanish *conquistadores* were establishing themselves in the Americas. With them they took their horses, a species that had been extinct in the New World for eight to ten thousand years. They also took their systems of horsemanship and training, and their equipment.

All three survive today and flourish if in only modified forms in the art and culture of the Western rider of California and Mexico.

In its true Western context, the hackamore comprises a heavy, braided rawhide noseband, shaped like an old-fashioned tennis racquet, plus various accompaniments. The noseband or *bosal* (*bosalillo*) is made so that there is a large, firm 'heel' knot at the rear that will lie between and behind the lower jawbones. The *bosal* is secured to the head by means of a lightweight *latigo* head stall. This can be kept in position by a slit made in the leather at an appropriate point so that it can be slipped over one ear, or the fitting can be made more secure by the addition of a *cavesada* (browband).

Attached to the heel knot is a heavy plaited rope rein called a *mecate*, which is made from mane hair, and a *fiador* made from the same material or from cotton. The *fiador* is a sort of throatlatch that is also attached to the heel knot, in order to fix its position to some degree and to prevent it from bumping against the lower jawbones while the horse is moving. The *mecate* is fitted to the heel knot by a system of 'wraps', which, if carefully adjusted, produce an extraordinarily delicate balance in the *bosal*, the weight of the reins and the heel knot acting as a counter-balance to the heavy nosepiece that lies some 5 cm (2 in) above the end of the nasal cartilage. The cheeks of the bosal slope downwards to the curb groove, behind and below which lies the heel knot.

At rest, or as long as the horse carries its head acceptably, a matter that can be adjusted by the number of 'wraps' taken round the heel knot, neither nosepiece nor heel are in contact, only the cheeks of the *bosal* lightly touch the sides of the face. When the hand is raised, a momentary restraint is applied to the nose, encouraging the horse to 'tuck in', i.e. retract the nose. Conversely, when the horse raises its head beyond the limits decreed by the adjustment, the nosepiece comes into contact to correct the head position. Meanwhile, the heel knot, operating between and against the jawbones, acts in opposition to prevent overbending and to discourage evasion of the nose pressure. What is thus created is a precision instrument capable of an adjustment so fine as to be unthinkable in the conventional European bridle.

Directional changes are made by the rein, held initially in both hands, being carried out to the side required and then supported by the opposite rein laid on the neck. Changes of direction are always accompanied by an appropriate and simultaneous shift of the rider's weight. Later the rein is held in one hand and laid against the neck on the side opposite to that to which the turn is to be made.

The fully schooled hackamore horse performs the movements required of it in a state of constant balance and usually at high speed. Furthermore, it executes the sliding stops, the pivots (the equivalent of the dressage pirouette but not, of course, quite the same movement), the sharp turns and the rein-back on a looping rein without its mouth ever being touched.

The ultimate refinement involves the transition to the potentially fearsome, long-cheeked, high-ported curb (spade) bit. This transition is made via lighter *bosals*, through a two-rein *bosal* (a lighter hackamore fitted with thin rein ropes) until eventually control passes to the bit, lightly supported by a *bosal* of the very slimmest proportions. Finally, the finished horse performs in the bit alone, without the assistance of any sort of noseband, and on a floating rein that exerts minimal pressure on the mouth. Reins may be weighted by small, decorative pieces of metal, but the ideal is for the horse to be ridden on the weight of a rawhide rein no more than 6 mm (¼ in) wide – the apotheosis of a classical tradition now lost to Europe.

The Thinking Bit

This heading refers to the Wellep bit, which, although its first production was withdrawn because of a technical failing, could claim to be 'a new concept in bitting'. That early fault has now been overcome and in time we may all have to reconsider the whole subject of bitting and review the existing rules as laid down by the current governing bodies. Would it, indeed, be possible to retain rulings relative to bitting based on a 400-year-old system of mechanics if there was a modern alternative that was not only more effective but more comfortable for the horse and reduced a hundred-fold the risk of damage to the mouth?

I have considered the Wellep separately, for the very good reason that it does not fall easily into any one of the accepted bitting groups.

It is now accepted by at least part of the riding public that the carriage of the horse is largely dependent upon the effectiveness of the rider's legs, seat, etc., and far less upon the type of bit being operated by the hand. None the less, however expertly the body aids are applied, their effect is reduced if the bit, the last link in the chain of aids, is not commensurately accurate. At best the conventional bit is less than precise and it is probable that it never achieves total constancy in its action. For that

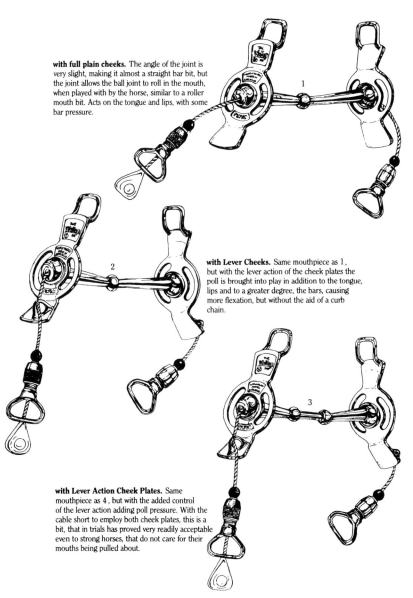

with full plain cheeks. The angle of the joint is very slight, making it almost a straight bar bit, but the joint allows the ball joint to roll in the mouth, when played with by the horse, similar to a roller mouth bit. Acts on the tongue and lips, with some bar pressure.

with Lever Cheeks. Same mouthpiece as 1, but with the lever action of the cheek plates the poll is brought into play in addition to the tongue, lips and to a greater degree, the bars, causing more flexation, but without the aid of a curb chain.

with Lever Action Cheek Plates. Same mouthpiece as 4, but with the added control of the lever action adding poll pressure. With the cable short to employ both cheek plates, this is a bit, that in trials has proved very readily acceptable even to strong horses, that do not care for their mouths being pulled about.

Some of the Wellep pattern bits as described in the Wellep brochure. The bit has yet to be perfected but it probably constitutes 'a new concept in bitting'

reason any bitting innovation that claims to eradicate imprecision and provide greater comfort for the horse, while also
allowing more effective use of the hand, has to be given serious
consideration.

The Wellep makes use of pressures that have long been
appreciated, although in this case they are combined ingeni-
ously in a single mouthpiece and can be applied with an almost
exact precision by educated hands.

It is, indeed, a near-perfectly engineered piece of equipment,
unapproachable in that context by any other product. The
mouthpiece is connected to the cheek plates (of original design)
by ball and socket joints, but the feature of the bit that has
resulted in it being described as 'revolutionary' is the cable that
passes through the jointed mouthpiece, at either end of which
rein attachment rings are fitted. This cable, the length of which
is adjustable, fulfils in a quite remarkable way the classical
concept of the continuous loop from one hand to the other.
This means that it should be possible for even an averagely
competent rider to feel with one hand the actions of the other.
A closing of the fingers of the left hand, for instance, is
transmitted to the right hand. The degree of sensitivity and the
directness of the action are controlled by the length of the cable.
A shorter cable gives greater sensitivity while a long cable makes
the action less direct and is for that reason recommended for
novice riders whose hands may still be unsteady.

To obtain a little pressure on the poll, in order to encourage
flexion at that point, the bit employs a 'lever' cheekpiece; in fact
the 'lever' is no more than a steel loop on the lower cheek,
through which the cable passes. Poll pressure is made easier by
the ability of each cheekpiece to rotate independently on its
own ball joint.

The cheeks themselves are shaped to the contours of the face
and, because of their construction, can accommodate any
variety of structure. Pressure on one rein assists a lateral
movement of the head through the increased pressure of the
opposite cheek on the side of the face.

The mouthpieces in the Wellep range are likely to vary from
the straight bar, acting principally on the tongue, to the double-
jointed spatula type, which, when used with lever cheeks, is a

pretty powerful instrument; although because of its construction, which gives, I think, a very high degree of comfort, it
would not cause a strong-pulling horse to intensify its efforts.

Part of the bit's success, I believe, is that it is suspended in the
mouth rather than resting on it. This is the principle employed
in the very successful 'hanging snaffles' exemplified by the Fillis
bradoon. Of equal importance, in those bits with a jointed
mouthpiece, is that the cable maintains a constant position of
the bit in the mouth and at the same time limits its movement so
that there is no possibility of the bit sliding from side to side. It
is therefore impossible to produce the punishing so-called
'nutcracker' action of the conventional snaffle across the tongue
and bars of the lower jaw, nor, of course, can the joint ever bear
upon the roof of the mouth – something that can happen in
certain mouth formations. The fact that the bit is suspended
allows it to be adjusted higher in the mouth and it will thus also
discourage a horse from getting its tongue over the mouthpiece.

This is a 'thinking' bit, by which I mean that it demands the
rider's concentration. As it is early days yet for this bit, there
may still be reservations to express but there seems no doubt
that the Wellep bit will give all serious riders much food for
thought. Of course, one has to reiterate that any bit, even this
one, is only as good as the legs, seat and hands behind it;
however, some bits can do more for you than others.

4: Auxiliaries – Martingales and Nosebands

The purpose of martingales and nosebands is:
1 To support the bit by preventing the horse from evading its intended action;
2 To strengthen the action and/or add further to it.

It is indeed possible for the effect of the bit to be quite radically altered by the addition of either a noseband or a martingale.

In every instance auxiliary aids fulfil their purpose by placing or even fixing the head so that the bit acts to full advantage on the mouth.

The most straightforward control of the head position is that offered by the *standing martingale*, a piece of equipment used extensively between the wars but now much out of favour. It is a strong adjustable strap with a loop at one end that allows it to be fitted to the rear of a plain cavesson noseband. The body of the martingale runs up between the forelegs from its attachment at the girth and always has a neck-strap to keep it in place.

The usual fitting adjustment recommended is for the end of the martingale to be in line with the wither. Clearly, the nose cannot then be thrown up above this point because of the restraint imposed by the noseband. That restraint is made more or less severe by the type of noseband used. A plain leather cavesson imposes minimal discomfort; one made of rope or fairly narrow rolled leather is obviously sharper in its action on the nose; while a noseband inset with a piece of metal may be regarded as being a very strong restraint and could cause callousing.

The martingale increases the rider's control significantly by allowing the bit to act across the lower jaw and preventing the nose from being carried above the level of the hand. (Before the Second World War, a 'stick' martingale was available as a training aid. In this the leather body of the martingale was replaced by a rigid cane running between the breast and the rear of the cavesson noseband. This arrangement allowed the head to be fixed precisely, the horse being quite unable to evade the bit either by throwing its nose up to come 'above' the bit, or by tucking its nose into its chest to become overbent and 'behind' the bit.)

The argument against the standing martingale is that it restricts the horse when jumping. In fact, this is untrue. When jumping, the horse's head and neck are stretched forwards and downwards, not upwards. If that is not the case then some pretty intensive reschooling is required and perhaps some riding lessons too. If the martingale is adjusted to the recommended length, there should be no restriction on the extension of the neck, although, clearly, that would not be the case if the martingale was adjusted too tightly.

In a strengthened, reinforced form the standing martingale is still virtually obligatory in the control of the polo pony. It is occasionally seen in the hunting field and if, in that context, it prevents the rider receiving a bloody nose as a result of a violent

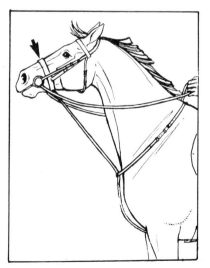

The standing martingale, now much out of favour except on the polo field, acts upon the nose via the cavesson noseband

Proof that the standing martingale does not restrict the extension of the neck

blow from the horse's head, and if, by increasing control, the possibility of an even more serious accident is avoided, then there can be no criticism of its use, for it achieves those objects without imposing pain. In other fields, however, the general disapproval of the standing martingale precludes its use.

The **running martingale**, although acting directly on the mouth rather than on the less sensitive nose, finds greater general acceptance.

This martingale divides into two branches at the breast, each one culminating in a ring through which the rein is passed. Like the standing martingale, it should be adjusted in line with the wither so as not to make an angle in the rein between hand and mouth. Should the horse raise its head above the permitted level, the movement is corrected by the martingale rings causing the bit to exert downward pressure, via the rein to which they are attached, across the lower jaw. Control is then increased and should the martingale be adjusted a hole or two tighter, the restraining action becomes stronger.

For safety's sake, the rein used with a running martingale should be fitted with 'stops' to prevent the rings sliding forwards and perhaps becoming caught in the rein fastening or, which is worse, over a tooth. If that should happen the horse could very well come over backwards.

Both martingales employ a neck strap – the rider's most convenient grab handle in any sort of emergency.

A horse ridden in a double bridle should not need the addition of a running martingale. However, should one be fitted it should logically be on the curb rein, the purpose of which is to lower the head. In the past, martingales intended for use with double bridles were made with a small triangular fitting that had a roller to run on the rein and prevent it from being twisted.

If one uses a running martingale for jumping schooling, the best and again the most logical pattern is the **pulley** type, in which the rings are set on a cord passing through a pulley at the top of the body strap. The advantage of this is that it allows for the lateral movement of the head and swift changes of direction

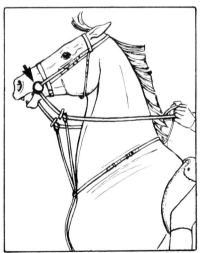

The far more popular running martingale relies for its effect upon exerting pressure across the lower jaw

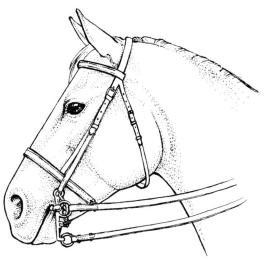

A cavesson noseband worn with a Pelham bridle. It is possible to obtain a partial closure of the mouth if the noseband is fitted snugly, otherwise its effect is no more than cosmetic

without causing restriction to the mouth on the opposite side. With an ordinary running martingale, a sharp turn to the right puts an opposite pressure, via the ring, on the left side of the mouth. This is avoided by the up and down movement made possible by the pulley.

Nosebands

Four principal types of noseband are used to reinforce the action of the bit. Three of them are permitted under the rules of dressage: the cavesson, drop and Flash and, indeed, the use of one of these is obligatory with a snaffle bridle. The Grakle, sometimes called the figure eight, is only permissible in horse trials and as it is specifically excluded from the items allowed under Paragraph 53 of the Dressage Rules, headed 'Gadgets', it must therefore be considered to be a gadget, not a proper noseband.

The plain, straightforward **cavesson** noseband, derived from the halter worn under the cavalry bridle, is no more than cosmetic in its effect when it is adjusted in accordance with the fitting recommended for a halter, i.e. allowing for the insertion of two fingers between the noseband and the head.

Dropped down a hole or two, however, and fastened more

tightly, it will bring about at least a partial closure of the mouth. (Closing the mouth so that the horse cannot evade the pressure of the bit is something of a preoccupation in modern riding. It was certainly not so in Britain in the past, when drop nosebands, the most effective method of preventing the mouth from being opened, were rarely used. British horsemen of the time held that little or no flexion was possible in a snaffle, that being reserved for the curb bit, to which the snaffle acted as a prelude. In Europe, however, the drop noseband had been regarded as integral to the snaffle bridle ever since the foundation of the early cavalry schools. Today, the drop noseband is regarded in that light almost everywhere and one wonders what sort of performances we would get without its help.)

A more effective cavesson pattern is the one that I call, probably incorrectly, the **Grandstand**, for no better reason than that it was a permanent feature of the bridle worn by Keith Luxford's champion cob of that name.

It differs from the ordinary cavesson by having a dee set on the rear strap on the near side. The point of the rear strap is passed through the dee and then doubled back to be fastened to a buckle sewn on the strap. Dropped down a hole, it can therefore be adjusted to close the mouth fairly effectively and without being fastened below the bit after the manner of the drop noseband – which in itself can be a source of resistance in some horses.

By encircling the nose and fastening below the bit the **drop noseband** does, of course, close the mouth almost completely. Its action, however, is more complex than that and its proper use produces flexion at the poll and, as far as the encircling strap allows, in the lower jaw.

If the mouth is prevented from opening, it follows that pressure from the rein will be transmitted to the nose, and as the nosepiece is fitted snugly and considerably lower than that of the cavesson noseband, it will cause the nose to be retracted and the face to be held nearer to the vertical with the poll flexed. Used firmly on a strongly pulling horse, this result is without doubt much assisted by the nose pressure, which causes momentary disruption to the breathing. Not unreasonably, the

The ubiquitous but less than perfectly understood drop noseband

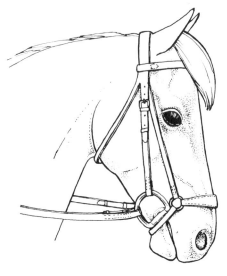

horse drops its nose, the bit acts decisively across the lower jaw, and the rider's control of the situation is increased. The horse cannot escape the pressure on its nose and across its mouth by opening the latter as this is held closed by the encircling nosepiece and rear fastening strap.

The legitimacy of such an action becomes questionable if there is a fault in the adjustment of the noseband or in its construction. The nosepiece should be fitted 6·5–7·5 cm (2½–3 in) above the nostrils on the end of the nasal bone. If it is adjusted lower than that, the horse will experience discomfort and have some difficulty in breathing.

If the rear strap of the noseband is made too short, the nosepiece will, inevitably, be positioned too low, and will obstruct the nasal passages.

The **Flash** noseband, as far as its origin is concerned, is a strange bedfellow among the equipment permitted under rules. It was originally a noseband devised for showjumping and, like so much else, took on the name of the horse that was among the first to wear it. It is, in fact, a strong cavesson, the original purpose of which was to provide an anchorage for a standing

The Flash noseband was originally intended for showjumping and it allowed a standing martingale to be attached to the cavesson portion

martingale. It is further strengthened by the addition of crossed straps, sewn to its centre, or otherwise attached, which can be adjusted under the bit to close the mouth. It is not, frankly, as effective in this last respect as the drop noseband but it avoids the nose pressure that is a feature of the latter. Used without a standing martingale, as it is today, it is not unreasonable nor unduly coercive to adjust the cavesson part of the noseband fairly snugly.

The noseband named after **Grakle**, winner of the 1931 Grand National, is, I believe, not so well understood, nor is it always made properly. Correctly constructed, the pressure point of the Grakle, which is sited at the place where the straps cross on the nose, can be adjusted in a way not open to the other patterns.

To work effectively, the straps should be shaped so that their highest point is where they join the headpiece. The top strap encircles the jaw above the bit, the lower straps below it, and they are held centrally and in close proximity by a short connecting strap lying behind and between the jaw bones. Without this small item the effective action that closes the jaws and prevents them from crossing is much reduced. The nose

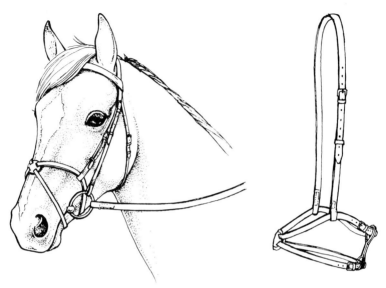

The Grakle (*left*) positions the point of pressure high on the nose at the point where the two straps intersect; (*right*) a correctly constructed Grakle. The majority of those available are not made in this way

pressure, because it is localised higher up the face, is less restrictive than that of the drop noseband and does not affect the breathing. Furthermore, the point of pressure can be adjusted up and down by moving the small nosepiece through which the straps are passed, thus increasing or decreasing the strength of the action. The Grakle does not enjoy complete acceptance in dressage competitions, possibly because, as a piece of racing equipment, it was not much known or used in the European training schools. On the other hand, it could be because so many of the patterns purporting to be Grakles have been made incorrectly.

There are, of course, other nosebands, which support the bit. A very strong, severe one is the **Puckle** or **Kineton** (invented by Mr Puckle who lived at Kineton). It does not close the mouth but it does put a lot of pressure on the nose. Two metal loops, fitted to the inside of the bit rings and behind the mouthpiece,

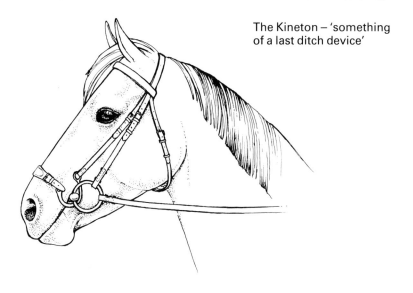

The Kineton – 'something of a last ditch device'

are connected to an adjustable nosepiece reinforced with a strip of shaped metal. Pressure on the rein produces a more or less powerful restraint on the nose, dependent upon the adjustment of the nosepiece. I think it falls into the 'brute strength' category. I have one in my tack room, but I cannot think how it got there nor can I recall it ever being used. In fact, the Kineton is something of a 'last ditch' device for the confirmed tearaway. It occasionally appears on the racecourse, not, of course, during the race but to ensure that a horse gets to the post without taking off irrevocably. Once at the start, it is removed.

A curiosity is the **Bucephalus**, or **Jobey** noseband (Bucephalus was the mount of Alexander the Great and his esteemed partner in all that legendary leader's many enterprises. Jobey, no doubt just as worthy, did not aspire to such heights.)

I doubt if the Bucephalus is ever used today. Certainly Jack Talbot-Ponsonby had one or two – but then he had the hands to

The simple Bucephalus noseband is used to strengthen a curb bit or a Pelham

match them. Its use is confined to either the curb of a double bridle or a Pelham and in this last context it is a useful aid in polo.

The Bucephalus is no more than a swollen, padded strap tapering at each end to a small metal dee. At the centre of the nosepiece is a small strap and buckle, used to secure the device to a cavesson noseband. The ends of the strap are passed round the jaws so that the off-side dee fastens to the near-side curb hook of the bit and the near-side dee to the off-side hook. In this way pressure on the nose reinforces the usual pressures exerted elsewhere by the curb.

5: The Conformation of the Mouth

Much lip service is paid to the fitting of the saddle and sometimes riders and saddlers will conscientiously measure and attempt to fit the saddle to the horse's back. The end result may or may not be entirely satisfactory but a gesture has, at least, been made and an awareness revealed of the necessity for a well-fitted saddle.

Every manual that I have ever read exhorts me to pick out my horse's feet twice daily. I have yet to meet one that instructs me to inspect my horse's mouth on the same basis, and have never seen one that advised me to study the horse's mouth before selecting a bit that will be suitable for it. I suspect that nine bits out of ten are imposed upon the horse's mouth without much thought being given to their suitability and fitting. In consequence, the bit chosen may conform very well to current fashion and the dictates of the riding schools but that is no guarantee that it will conform in equal measure to the horse's mouth – surely the prime consideration and requirement.

The parts of the mouth that determine the choice of bit, particularly when it comes to a curb bit, are these: The *bars*, those narrow ridges of bone, thinly covered with gum, that lie between the incisor teeth (the biters) and the molars (the grinders); the *tongue*; the *tongue channel* or *groove*; the *lips*; the *curb groove*; the *roof of the mouth*. The *teeth* must also be examined as their condition has a direct influence on bitting practice.

However, before any of these things can be examined, it is first necessary to persuade the horse to open its mouth. If it is possible to train a horse to move sideways, to jump fences from a trot or to lift up a foot in response to the command 'Pick it up' (or even 'Put it *down*', as long as that command is always given

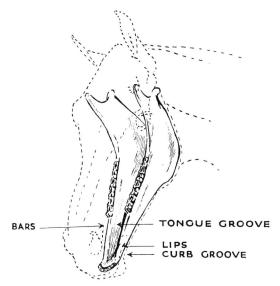

BARS

TONGUE GROOVE

LIPS
CURB GROOVE

A diagram of the mouth showing the principal parts involved in the art of bitting

consistently and corresponds with the action required), it ought to be just as easy to teach the horse to open its mouth on request. Try, if you like, 'Say aah', but, to start with, accompany this by assisting the opening with your fingers.

Place the first finger and thumb round the lower jaw, the two being inserted very gently into the mouth on either side so that they lie over the bars. If you are gentle, the horse will oblige by opening its mouth. If, on the other hand, you place your spare hand firmly over its nostrils, or attempt to seize the jaw in a vice-like grip, the reaction will be quite the opposite of what is wanted.

When the mouth is opened, take the tongue, again very quietly, in your spare hand and bring it out to the side. The horse will not, and cannot, bite you, had, indeed, such an ignoble thought ever entered its head, and it is far too sensible to attempt to bite off its own tongue. However, should the horse show signs of alarm and try to pull away, *let go* of the tongue at once – hanging on could do irreparable damage. If that sounds too difficult, invest in a Swales veterinary gag, which is easy to

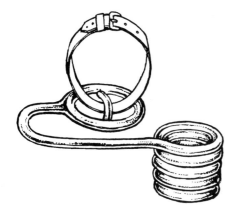

Swales Gag. Fasten the strap to the headcollar, place the gag in the mouth and one is then able to inspect the mouth at leisure

handle and keeps the mouth open so that it can be inspected at leisure.

If that exercise is carried out twice a day, and the horse rewarded intelligently for its co-operation, it should be possible within a week to get it to open up on request.

Once the mouth is open, a cursory examination reveals the presence of teeth, bars and tongue. Look a little closer and it is possible to see the formation of the tongue channel and the roof of the mouth.

Teeth

The mature horse (a six year old) will have a 'full mouth', i.e. a complete set of permanent teeth. This will comprise twelve molar teeth and six incisor teeth in each jaw, these two groups of teeth being separated by the area of gum that we know as the bars of the mouth. In the male horse, an additional 'tush' grows behind the incisors; perhaps, long ago, it had a purpose, but it is now surplus to normal requirements. Both males and females sometimes develop wolf teeth, which appear in the upper jaw just in advance of the molars. Not only do they have no useful function, but they can also be an unmitigated nuisance. They can certainly interfere with the bitting arrangements, causing discomfort and a notable unsteadiness in the mouth, and so they are best removed. This operation is easily accomplished by a veterinary surgeon, but the condition has first to be detected and that involves regular inspection of the mouth.

It will also be evident that the upper jaw is larger than the lower one, and a closer look will reveal that the molars of the upper jaw grow *downwards and outwards* while those of the lower jaw grow *upwards and inwards.* As a result of this conformation, the enamel on the outside of the top molars and the inside of the lower ones tends not to receive the same wear as the rest of the tooth. The edges of the teeth can therefore become very sharp and cause pain and eating difficulties. For this reason, the teeth need to be checked as part of the daily inspection by the owner and at least once a year by a veterinary surgeon who will rasp them smooth if and when it is necessary to do so. He or she will also check for teeth that have become split or decayed.

The consequences of neglecting the teeth can be serious and out of all proportion to the time and expense incurred in keeping them in good order. Sharp teeth may cause acute discomfort by lacerating the inside of the cheek or the tongue, or both. Decayed or split teeth will cause similar discomfort. Such a poor state of the teeth interferes with the mastication of food; it gives rise to irritability and when the horse is ridden it may express its resentment through all sorts of resistances. When these occur, the owner who is unaware of the condition inside the horse's mouth, may be tempted to resort to a change of bit or some other piece of extraneous equipment in an effort to correct the horse's behaviour. Both, of course, will be wholly non-productive and possibly expensive, too. In the process, the horse's temper is unlikely to improve; it may become soured and the resistances could become habitual, making a cure more difficult to effect.

Teething problems are bound to occur with young horses as permanent teeth take the place of milk teeth. As with the human child, the process is accompanied by some irritability and the discomfort of temporarily inflamed gums. If a young horse is ridden while permanent teeth are erupting, it may very well indulge in head-shaking to obtain relief. The answer, as long as one appreciates what is happening, is to take the horse out of work for a day so that the bridle will not aggravate the condition, and to rub the gums with tincture of myrrh or oil of cloves, as you would with a child. (Good Scotch whisky works just as well, but can probably be put to better use.) Again, the solution depends upon regular inspection.

Bars

In young, unbroken, Thoroughbred-type horses whose mouths have not been subjected to a bit, the bars appear as narrow, sharp ridges of bone, thinly covered with flesh. They are *exceedingly sensitive.*

Rough handling of the bit will wear away the ridge. It becomes flatter and may become covered with a calloused growth of skin. It then becomes less sensitive and the horse will be described by the species responsible for the condition as being 'hard-mouthed'. It is possible for the flesh on the bar to be cut to the extent that a hole is made in which food can lodge and then, of course, infection can occur. Where damage to the bars is severe, it is even possible for the bone of the bars to be splintered. But, of course, you won't know anything about that, or the other conditions, unless you look into the mouth.

On the other hand, flatter and more heavily fleshed bars will be found in less highly bred animals, often those cobby types that may have a short, thick jaw formation. It follows that flat bars of this sort, or those that are permanently calloused, will be somewhat less sensitive to direct bit pressures than the sharp, thinly covered sort.

Tongue

The tongue varies considerably in shape and size, from large and fleshy and appearing to be too big for the mouth, to one that is much thinner and narrower. Which bit, either curb or snaffle, will suit best depends to an extent upon the type of bar accompanying the tongue formation and whether the horse will accept tongue pressure.

Usually, a big fleshy tongue will take pressure, but not always. If the bars will accept bit contact, a bigger port is needed to accommodate a larger tongue. The opposite extreme, a thin tongue, causes its own problems as it does nothing towards protecting the bars. It demands a mild bit, a mullen mouth, possibly an inverted mouth (i.e. an arch turned upside down) or a bit from the German range that is manufactured from soft flexible plastic.

Tongue groove

The tongue groove can add to our problems. If it is too shallow, it does not allow sufficient room for the tongue to lie comfortably in it. The tongue may then be subjected to undue pressure. Very often the reason why horses get into the habit of putting the tongue over the bit is in order to avoid the discomfort of the pressure being put on it.

Lips

The lips are very easily chafed or bruised at their edges and may become calloused.

The principal causes are:

1   Too broad a bit;
2   Too wide a bit;
3   Pinching caused by wear around the hole through which a loose ring passes.

The remedy is very obvious.

Curb groove

The curb groove is the critical area just below the junction of the two jaw branches. The bone at this point is smooth and covered with gristle that is comparatively insensitive. This is the area over which the curb chain should fit *exactly*. For this to happen, the bit must be constructed to allow such a fitting and the chain adjusted accordingly.

Above this point the jaw bones change shape and become sharp ridges covered only with thin, sensitive skin. If the chain rides upwards, it can chafe, bruise and be generally damaging to the skin and the bone beneath.

Roof of the mouth

Finally, it is worth looking at the roof of the mouth. Sometimes it is lower than normal and may then come into contact with the port of a curb bit or the joint of a plain snaffle, particularly if the latter is too big for the mouth – neither reason is acceptable and both cause discomfort and provoke an understandable resistance as a result.

Regular inspection of the mouth will confirm that the bit that is being used is the correct one for the individual, or it will reveal, unmistakably, its shortcomings. Corrective measures can then be taken. It can often be a salutary and humbling experience to examine a horse's mouth after a day's hunting or perhaps after a cross-country event. One would be ashamed if one's horse showed whip marks on its quarters and flanks. A bruised mouth is equally reprehensible but, of course, it cannot be seen by anyone – except, one hopes, by yourself.

Let Major Francis Dwyer, Major of Hussars in the Imperial Austrian Service, have the last, or almost the last, word.

The whole art of bitting consists, so far as the mouthpiece goes, in determining how much of the pressure shall fall on the tongue and how much on the bars, and we are thus enabled, by means of an almost infinite system of gradations, to obtain exactly the degree of action required in each particular instance . . .

Quite so, but you will not get near to that ideal until the mouth is inspected as frequently as the feet are picked out.

6: Fitting the Bridle

A bridle comprises the leather portions: head, cheeks, nose-band, reins and, in the case of a double bridle, the sliphead from which is suspended the bradoon, and the bit or bits. The general rules of fitting apply equally to all types and the object in all respects is to ensure that the horse is entirely comfortable.

In the fitting of any bridle, the two critical points are the browband, or 'front', and the throatlatch (spelt that way but pronounced 'throat*lash*').

Too short a browband will pull the bridle head forward so that it presses up against the back of the ears. This is irritating to the horse and is a frequent cause of head-shaking, which is quite likely to become habitual. Apart from the habit being annoying, it makes any proper action of the bit impossible. A browband fitted too high, so as to press against the base of the ears, even if it is otherwise sufficiently long, may also cause head-shaking to develop. As a rough guide, allow for the insertion of one finger between the browband and the forehead and for the browband to be positioned 25 mm (1 in) lower than the base of the ears.

A throatlatch adjusted too tightly, as well as being uncomfortable, can restrict the breathing and will discourage the horse from flexing at the poll. Allow for the insertion of three fingers between it and the gullet.

It is usual to have the buckles of the cheekpieces, which obviously have to be level, in line with or just below the eye, with the buckles fastening the headpiece of the noseband similarly positioned. The buckle of the double bridle sliphead lies level with that of the noseband and fastens on the off side of the head.

(The adjustment of nosebands has been discussed already, see Chapter 4.)

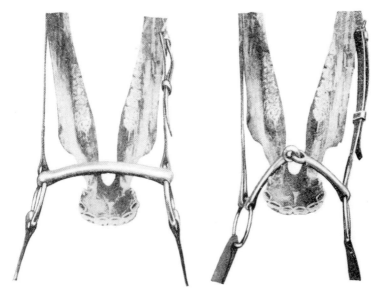

The action of the snaffle across the lower jaw. It can be seen why it is so necessary for the bit to fit perfectly and to be positioned centrally in the mouth

The Snaffle Bit

A snaffle of any type should correspond as nearly as possible to the width of the mouth. It should, therefore, fit closely to the cheeks, the butt end of a loose-ring snaffle projecting on each side by no more than 13 mm (½ in). It is easier to obtain a snug fit with an eggbutt or a full-cheek than with a loose ring, as with these forms there is no need to worry about the lips being pinched where the loose ring passes through the hole in the mouthpiece.

A snaffle that is too narrow will obviously pinch the cheeks. Most snaffles, however, fail because they are too wide for the mouth (probably because the owner is anxious to avoid fitting too narrow a bit).

If the bit is too wide, it will slide across the mouth, exaggerating its action on one side and possibly causing bruising to the tongue, bars and lips on that side. If it is adjusted too low and used in conjunction with a drop noseband, a jointed snaffle may bear painfully at its joint on the roof of the mouth, a contact that is intensified by the noseband preventing the mouth from being opened. It may also knock up against the incisor teeth, something that will also occur in a snaffle of the correct width if it is adjusted too low in the mouth.

The bit is correctly fitted when the corners of the lips are just wrinkled.

A snaffle bit with a fairly pronounced curve to both halves of the mouthpiece conforms better to the shape of the lower jaw than those that are straighter in the mouth. Generally, bits made 50–100 years ago are of a better shape than modern ones. It is, however, still possible to find well-curved bits and the difference in the way the horse carries such a bit and responds to it is noticeable.

The Curb Bit

The curb bit used in a double bridle lies in the mouth below the bradoon, the latter being fitted as the snaffle.

If it is important that the snaffle correspond to the width of the mouth, it is absolutely essential that the curb should do so exactly. The fit should be as close to the outside of the lips as possible without actually pressing on them.

Should the bit be too big (and, again, very many are too wide in the mouth) it will be very easy for it to become displaced to one side or the other. When that happens, the bar on the side affected may come under the port, or partially so, in which case all the pressure goes onto the tongue and the corner of the port will bear most painfully on the bar. The action is then interrupted and uneven. That, in itself, will be reflected in the carriage of head and mouth and, in turn, transmitted to the movement, which becomes unlevel.

Too tight a bit fitting is just as bad, as the inside of the lips will be pushed over the bars and will be bruised and pinched by the pressure of the mouthpiece.

It is easier to fit a fixed cheek bit more closely than one with a slide cheek. Fitted too closely, a sliding cheek increases the

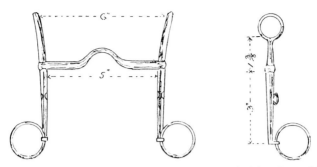

A correctly constructed curb bit as recommended by Capt. M. H. Hayes in his book *Riding and Hunting*. The cheeks incline outwards above the mouthpiece to conform with the shape of the face and to prevent chafing

chance of the lips being pinched between the moving cheek and the hole in the mouthpiece through which it passes.

A failing in modern bits is the vertical construction of the cheeks, which makes no allowance for the slight swell of the face above the lips. If the top of the cheek, above the mouthpiece, forms a gentle outward curve there is no chance of it pressing uncomfortably against the face. Should the conformation of the horse's face make it necessary however, this deficiency can be made good by gently bending the eyes outwards, having first secured them in the jaws of a vice.

The positioning of the mouthpiece is obviously of paramount importance. It needs to lie between the tush (in the case of a gelding) and the molars and, ideally, is equidistant from the two. The military ruling was 'one inch [25 mm] above the tush of a horse and two inches [50 mm] above the corner tooth of a mare'. The bit must not, of course, hit up against the tush, but the military instruction quoted may place the mouthpiece just a little too high. Tushes do vary in their position and the lower ones do not always correspond with those in the upper jaw. One has, therefore, to fit the bit according to the conformation of the individual horse rather than the rule.

A valuable guide, however, which also puts the curb chain in the right place is to '*place the mouthpiece on that part of the bars exactly opposite the chin groove*'.

The adjustment of the curb chain can be made by tilting the

cheek of the bit so that the chain is operative when the cheek reaches a 45-degree angle – or less if you want a more immediate response, a minimal poll pressure and are convinced of the gossamer-like nature of your hands.

The curb chain is always kept in place by a lip-strap that will, so I am assured by the authorities of the last century, also prevent the cheeks from 'swinging forward and becoming reversed, as they might do, were it absent, in the event of the horse throwing up his head'. Captain M. H. Hayes, the author of those words, continued: 'When the cheeks are thus reversed the rider will have but little control over his mount.' I believe him and am thankful that I have never witnessed a bit reversal!

The Pelham

Like most compromises the Pelham satisfies neither party entirely. Other than with a Rugby Pelham, the longer length of cheek above the mouthpiece pulls the curb chain upwards out of the curb groove and that movement is intensified when the Pelham is fitted high enough in the mouth to give a snaffle action when the top rein is applied. As the bit is a compromise, its position in the mouth must follow the same road. In the instance of the Pelham, one can do no better than follow the military rule as far as possible, but one should also fit the curb chain with a rubber guard or use an elastic one.

The cheeks above the mouth cause even more problems if they are not inclined outwards, away from the face.

The Nose Bridle

This has to be fitted very closely if it is not to rub the nose and the nosepiece should never be less than 76 mm (3 in) above the nostrils. Ideally, the height of the nosepiece should be altered each day in order to prevent continual pressure in one place from callousing the nose. Both nosepiece and back strap, as well as the area at the side of the face with which the top ends of the cheeks come into contact, require to be very well padded if chafing is to be avoided.

A parting thought from Major Dwyer: '. . . nothing can be

more certain than that the best bitting in the world is wholly
useless, nay, sometimes dangerous, in bad, that is to say, heavy
or rude hands'.

7: Buying a Bridle

The best advice is to buy the best, which will not, of course, be cheap.

The leather should have 'substance', i.e. a good thickness, which will increase its capacity to carry the grease dressings that are its strength and that keep it supple. It should always be a little greasy, never dry, and should feel firm in the hand, not soft and pappy. When it is cut from a top-quality butt, the back of the leather, the 'flesh' side, will be smooth, not rough and fibrous. The 'grain' side, the outer surface, should also be quite smooth and when bent in the fingers there should be no wrinkling or bubbling of the top skin. A good bridle has the edges of the leather bevelled and rubbed smooth and the keepers (the loops through which the points of the cheek straps, throatlatch, etc. are passed) will be properly shaped and blocked out. The stitching, too, is an indication of the quality. The waxed thread, with which a good bridle is sewn, is recognised by its faintly yellow colour.

If a plain cavesson noseband is purchased, buy one in which the headpiece is slotted through the nosepiece, not sewn to it. The nosepiece then hangs better and does not droop at the front.

On a double or Pelham bridle, the top, bradoon, rein needs to be 3 mm (⅛ in) wider than the curb rein so that it is easy to differentiate between the two. The reins on a good bridle always culminate in a small buckle and strap fastening at the hand part. It is no more than an extra, mostly unused convenience, rather like the cigar lighter fitted in the car of a non-smoker, but it remains the hallmark of a quality bridle. Cheap bridles dispense with this nicety, the rein ends simply being sewn together. (In the days when the horse world was much concerned about being 'correct', a bridle would have been deemed to be fitted incorrectly unless the buckle was on the near-side rein with the point of the strap on the opposite side. To undo the rein from the saddle, should one have ever wished to do so, it was only necessary to free the point from the keeper with the left thumb and then unfasten the buckle with the right hand – a strange little convention of no practical use, this probably had a military origin, the ruling being made in the interests of uniformity.)

As it is possible to cut only four top-class bridles from a single hide and only from that part, known as the butts, on either side of the backbone, it is not difficult to understand why a quality bridle is an expensive item, even though, if given proper care, it will last a lifetime and even improve with age. (A pair of butts is cut from a full hide. The butts are the central portion excluding the shoulder and the flank and belly hide.)

There is nothing like a really good leather rein that comes comfortably to the hand and I would not wish to contemplate the time when a gleaming leather bridle did not hang in my tack room. To be practical, however, maintaining such a bridle in pristine condition is a time-consuming if pleasurable occupation. For that reason, a synthetic bridle made of nylon web, or web covered in soft plastic, should not be despised. It has a useful role to fulfil in the activities of the modern rider. Its strength is undeniable, the metal fastenings are usually excellent, it is well made and finished and, perhaps above all, it is easy to clean. All that is needed is a sponge over after use. As a day-to-day exercise bridle, it is unrivalled and it allows the splendid leather creation to be reserved for high days and holidays.

Cleaning

At the basis of leather maintenance is an understanding of the properties and nature of the material.

In brief the 'grain' side of leather (the outside) has undergone a dressing process that seals the pores on that side and renders it almost waterproof. The 'flesh' side has not received this sealing to any extent and the pores of the leather are open and ready both to receive and lose the nourishment that is necessary to keep the leather soft, supple and alive. The grease content of leather can be regarded as its life blood. A percentage of this constituent is regularly lost in general use and in order for the leather to retain its suppleness, this grease has to be just as regularly replaced.

Leather has two principal enemies (if we disregard human neglect). They are water and heat. Water, particularly when it is hot, melts and removes the fat; heat dries it out. In both instances the leather is left hard and brittle right up to the point where it can be snapped in two in the fingers. Leather loses its fat content, little by little, when in use because of the heat and sweat generated by the horse's body. When dry, the sweat can be seen as a white deposit blocking the pores on the flesh side of the leather.

To clean a bridle it is first necessary to take it to pieces, attending to each part separately. First sponge off the sweat deposits and any dirt that may be on the grain surface. Dry the leather and then use a glycerine-based saddle soap or something similar. If you have a bar of soap rather than a tin or tub, dip the end in water and then rub the sponge on the soap instead of trying to work with an impossibly wet and lathery sponge. Rub the soap well into the leather, paying particular attention to the flesh side. Finish off by polishing with a slightly damp chamois leather.

At least once a week, apply the preparation of your choice (I use a beeswax and lanolin preparation) and rub it well into the flesh side with your fingers. It is very important to keep the leather well greased on the inside of the billets where the reins and cheekpieces are turned to fasten to the metal bit, as these are areas subject to the greatest wear.

There is now a legion of leather-cleaning preparations on the market to do the job better and in less time. Take advantage of them but go easy on the oils. It is just as easy to overfeed leather as to starve it. A surfeit of oils, which the leather is unable to absorb, causes loss of tenacity in the fibres. The leather becomes flabby and greasy and oozes oil unpleasantly, to the detriment of anything coming in contact with it.

Finally, wash the bits in warm water every day after use. To put a dirty bit into a horse's mouth is as bad as asking your guest to eat soup with a spoon caked in old dried food. Good horsemen and horsewomen just don't do it. Furthermore, do not wash your bits with soap or clean them with metal polish. Both taste unpleasant.

horsemen and horsewomen just don't do it. Furthermore, do not wash your bits with soap or clean them with metal polish. Both taste unpleasant.